All Together Now: Creating a Social Capital Mosaic

All Together Now: Creating a Social Capital Mosaic

Frances Ricks/Vanier Institute of the Family

Cover mosaic and book illustrations by
Sarah McCoubrey, Victoria, B.C.

Canadian Cataloguing in Publication Data

Main entry under title:
All together now

Copublished by: Vanier Institute of the Family.
Includes bibliographical references.
ISBN 1-55058-201-1

1. Human capital. 2. Community development. I. Ricks, Frances. II. Vanier Institute of the Family.
HN49.C6A44 1999   307.1'4   C99-910966-9

For additional copies of this book, contact:
Frances Ricks: (250) 721-7989

Published by:
FRANCES RICKS, VICTORIA, BRITISH COLUMBIA
VANIER INSTITUTE OF THE FAMILY, OTTAWA, ONTARIO

Editing and layout by:
Laura Bramly
SYNERGY COMMUNICATIONS
406-2560 Wark Street
Victoria, British Columbia V8T 4G8

Printed and bound in Canada by:
MORRISS PRINTING COMPANY LTD.
1745 Blanshard Street
Victoria, British Columbia V8W 2J8

This book is dedicated to the communities already involved in their transformation and to the communities which aspire to undertake this opportunity and challenge.

The Authors

Dr. Frances Ricks is a professor in the School of Child and Youth Care at the University of Victoria. She has been involved in aspects of organizational and community development since graduating from York University in 1972. She has long believed in individuals and communities living their dreams. *Gerard Bellefeuille* is a doctoral student in the School of Child and Youth Care at the University of Victoria. During his seven years as the Executive Director of the Awasis Agency of Northern Manitoba, he worked with Dr. Ricks on projects designed to increase social capital in the eighteen First Nations communities served by the Agency. He continues this work as a community development consultant to First Nations in Manitoba. *Jennifer Charlesworth* is a doctoral student in the School of Child and Youth Care at the University of Victoria. She has returned to her studies after many years of working in various communities in government services and continues community development work as a consultant. *Anne Field* is a Masters candidate in the School of Child and Youth Care at the University of Victoria. She has been a Child and Youth Care worker in community schools for many years and has maintained a relationship with Dr. Ricks since graduating from the School of Child and Youth Care in 1981.

This community of authors has over 100 years of experience in community work and community development. While working together from different locations across Canada, they have had the experience of creating and living their own Social Capital Mosaic.

Table of Contents

Preface...ix
Prologue...xiii

Part 1: In The Beginning: Assessing the Problem..........1
This Isn't Working 5
Objectification and Separation............................. 7
Competition and Protectionism 10
Having and Knowing are Learning Disabilities 12
Governance as Social Control 17
Simplification and Fragmentation 24

Part 2: Rethinking Community and Social Capital 31
What is Community? 32
Healthy Community is the Goal 33
A New Reality in Community 36
Principles and Values for a New Reality 39
An Overview of Social Capital 39
Social Capital Mosaic 43
When It Works... 43
More Capitals 45
Relational Factors in the Mosaic 49
In a Different Process 50
Create a Culture of Inquiry 51
All Together Now 53

Part 3: Living a Social Capital Mosaic 55
Personalization and Inclusion 56
Trusting Relationships —
    The Heart of the Social Capital Mosaic 60
Cooperation and Collaboration 71
Mutual Learning 80
Empowerment Through Governance 86

Part 4: Getting Started 95
The Process of Assessment, Reflection and Creation 95
Start Anywhere and Work with What You Have 102
Key Skills for Getting Started 103
Leadership.. 110
Creating Social Capital is Not Hard. It's Slow! 117
What's Your Story? 118

Appendix: Stories.. 119
Bibliography 137

Figures and Tables

Figure 1:   Values That Do Not Work 6

Figure 2:   Turfs and Social Issues 11

Figure 3:   Tame, Wicked, Messes,
            and Wicked Messes 26

Figure 4:   Ideas of Healthy Community 34

Figure 5:   A New Way of Thinking 37

Figure 6:   Community Conversations 38

Figure 7:   Values That Contribute to Social Capital 40

Figure 8:   Creating a Social Capital Mosaic 42

Figure 9:   Creating the Capitals 46

Figure 10: Culture of Inquiry 52

Figure 11: Living a Social Capital Mosaic 57

Figure 12: Human Capital Factors 60

Figure 13: Enhancing Levels of Capitals 62

Figure 14: Levels of Relationship 64

Figure 15: Trust in Creating Social Capital 69

Figure 16: Essential Conditions for People
            To Be Different in Community 70

Figure 17: Community-focussed vs.
            Community-driven 78

Figure 18: Community Learning Process 80

Figure 19: Speaking and Practicing Differently 82

Figure 20: The Community Design Process 96

Table 1:   Bureaucracy Model vs.
            Public Choice Model 88

Today you would be hard-pressed to read a newspaper, never mind a public policy paper, which doesn't look to communities as the answer. But to what question?

Julie White[1]

In Canada and elsewhere today, there is much talk of a renewed role for community as we confront the "crisis" and contraction of the Welfare State. Canadians speak with hope of community revitalization, civic renewal, and the capacity of the so-called Third Sector comprised of not-for-profit, voluntary, and charitable organizations. We look to community as a source of jobs, economic recovery, and provider of primary care. The capacity of communities is, it is thought, to be harnessed as a preferred and cost-effective alternative to the anonymity of the state and its bureaucracies and to the self-interest of the marketplace. And, beyond the instrumental motives of costs and efficiencies lies a search for societal redemption, a reaffirmation of values thought to have been eclipsed in an era of "expressive individualism" and a moral perspective emphasizing a renewed sense of belonging and shared values.

As citizens confronted too often by the indifference of others and ourselves, we are drawn to conversations that speak again of civic virtue and neighbourliness. We are awed by the commitment and capacity of neighbours and communities of strangers confronted by a flood in Manitoba or an ice storm that cripples Eastern Ontario and Western Quebec, or a fire that leaves a family homeless. These extraordinary events prompt extraordinary expressions of civic will and common purpose. Yet, why do these examples strike us as so extraordinary, so unusual, and so remarkable? This is an important question because it is precisely this civic commitment and capacity that we would hope to build upon and sustain on more than an episodic basis if we are to renew our communities and, in the process, renew ourselves.

In this book, Frances Ricks, Jennifer Charlesworth, Gerard Bellefeuille, and Anne Field extend an invitation. We are invited to join in their search to discover the essential foundations of community. Their examination of social capital is distinguished from much that is written today

[1] Julie White (1997). "Building Caring Communities: Five Capacities that Build Communities and Ten Things Funders Can Do to Support Them." Toronto: Trillium Foundation, p.1.

precisely because they do not take community for granted as though it were a perennial that blooms anew each and every year without much care and attention. They know that the recent "rediscovery" of community is all too often naive and expedient. They know that it is not possible to simply turn on a "thousand points of civic light." They are, rather, more respectful of the time, energy, and resources that must be invested in building the foundation of the lives we live together in our homes and our communities.

Like the artist who draws our gaze toward a part of the visual landscape previously overlooked, the authors invite us to recover an appreciation of the energy, shared vision, and potential that reside within a meeting of parents, a school play, a neighbourhood barbecue, a community conference convened by members of a Northern reserve, or a drop-in centre for parents.

Each author has worked in the child, youth, family, and community service field. Their experience serves as an essential resource from which they both question conventional community development strategies and go on to isolate and identify the elements of what they call the "Social Capital Mosaic." Illustrated throughout by real stories of what works and what doesn't, this book opens up for discussion topics and ideas usually only encountered in conversations around the water cooler or in the hallways between workshops at professional conferences. It is there most often that we hear talk about how our best and most humane intentions are perversely thwarted by the "systems" of service and care within which we work.

The authors have found that most people with whom they have lived and worked want the same things: a safe community, a good place to raise kids, meaningful educational and work opportunities, decent and affordable housing, nutritious food and good health care, equality and choice, connection with others. Yet curiously, the systems of support we have created are more accountable to existing policies, procedures, legislation, and fiscal constraints than to these stated needs and aspirations. Unable to reflect upon and recover the original sense of purpose with which we began our commitment to communities, we are disoriented.

There is no map to lead us out of the wilderness into the domain of the Social Capital Mosaic. Social capital per se, they suggest, is not one thing but rather is built upon distinct though intimately connected sets of economic, physical, human, environmental, and relational assets. For years and years, the distinction between that which is social and that which is economic has been known to limit our understanding and our options. Yet, the contention that the social and economic are one-in-the-same has served as little more than trite rhetoric without an appreciation of how each form of capital assumes value only as it adds to and contributes to the growth of the others.

The Social Capital Mosaic encompasses these assets and resides neither with the individual nor the collectivity. It is neither personal nor political. It is, rather, predicated upon the capacity and commitment of individuals to act with common purpose. The Social Capital Mosaic requires "personal" commitments to the "public good." Accordingly, the authors proceed to describe both the foundations of trust that lie at the "heart of the Social Capital Mosaic" as well as the forms of association and governance that can foster the growth of individuals, families, and communities.

Contrary to much popular opinion, families do not stand alone as independent building blocks — cornerstones — of society. Families do not thrive unless they are surrounded by communities that care deeply about them and are willing to invest in them. And, it is equally true that our communities cannot hope to survive much less thrive without the physical care, economic production, socialization, and education and, last but not least, the commitment, affection, trust, and love that family members ideally demonstrate to one another. The Social Capital Mosaic is built, the authors assert, by individuals who trust one another enough to open themselves to genuine questioning, inquiry, and learning. It takes people with various cognitive and organizational skills to be sure, but these attributes are not, in themselves, sufficient. To work well in community requires "emotional intelligence" and nurturing skills, an awareness of self and others, the capacity to express empathy, and to communicate effectively.

If it is trust that lies at the heart of the Social Capital Mosaic, it is within the family, whatever its shape or form, that the potential for trust, reciprocity, disciplining, self-restraint, and responsibility resides. It is our families that are the seedbeds of civic virtue. As Ernesto Cortes Jr. has said:

> Families teach the first lessons of relationship among persons, some of which are essential not only to private life but to public life as well. Within the family one learns to act upon others and to be acted upon. It is in the family that we learn to identify ourselves with others or fail to learn to love. It is in the family that we learn to trust others as we depend on them or learn to distrust them. We learn to hold ourselves accountable.[2]

For too long, we have taken too much for granted. We have taken our families for granted. We have taken our communities for granted. And now that we need both more than ever before, we must face the fact that we must invest anew in each. There is no recipe for social capital here. Rather what the authors provide is a much-improved list of ingredients that we must cultivate, assemble, and blend as we seek to renew the lives we live together.

Robert Glossop
Executive Director of Programs
Vanier Institute of the Family

---

[2] Ernesto Cortes Jr. (1996). Cited by Jean Bothke Elshtain in "Marriage in Civil Society." Family Affairs, vol. 7, no.1-2, p.3.

This book has been in the making for a very long time, not in a formal sense — it has been written only in the past year — but in an informal and evolutionary sense. It has evolved through our experiences, collectively close to one hundred years in the child, youth, family, and community service field. It has evolved through our mutual commitment to learning and growth and through reflection, dialogue, and practice. It has evolved through our commitment to partnerships and working together to find expression for our vision of a better way to make the world a better place. It is, in essence, lived social capital, and it is greater than any one of us. It is also, simply, a work in progress.

This book formally began to take shape in a conversation between Frances Ricks and Gerard Bellefeuille, long-standing partners in learning and building human and social capital. The conversation went something like this… "What if we could pull together examples of social capital in the making? What if we could incorporate these examples into a book and create a new understanding of how social capital works? What if we could use the book project itself to generate social capital?"

To widen the circle of inquiry into social capital, Frances tapped into the experiences and interests of Jennifer Charlesworth and Anne Field. The four of us have individually followed different paths in our practice, yet we collectively share a vision of health and wellbeing for all within communities. We have explored different ideas, theories, and prescriptions for change and found them to be wanting. The time had come to share with each other and with you, the reader, what we have come to believe and value, what we have learned and what we are learning about people and communities and community development:

- **Every community and community member has the capacity to be different**.
- **You can start anywhere and with whatever you have**.
- **Healthy communities and healthy individuals are interdependent**.
- **Respect for the dignity and worth of people promotes equal opportunities and access to resources**.

If you share these beliefs and values with us, then this book will be significant to you.

As we developed this book, we shared our stories and experiences and then asked questions. "What happened there? What made a difference? Why did this feel better than that? What got in the way? What helped?" We read the literature on social capital, community development, learning organizations, organizational development, leadership, and so on and then asked more questions. "Where does this idea/concept/framework/theory take us? Does this fit with our experience? How can we add to or work with this? What pieces fit together and how? How do we make this come alive?" We teased out the "big ideas" and began writing. We invite you to go through a similar process as you work through this book.

As we moved forward with the book, the image of a mosaic began to emerge. Many small pieces, each with their own integrity and value, can be artfully brought together to create something greater than the pieces. In this book, we present our ideas as pieces within a mosaic of social capital and suggest ways in which they have come together for us.

These may not be the only pieces, nor is this the only way to organize the pieces to create an understanding of the Social Capital Mosaic and how it works. We must be clear — this is not a prescriptive book. It will not tell you definitively which pieces to pick up, nor where and how to place them in order to build social capacity. It simply attempts to bring to light different aspects of the Social Capital Mosaic, which we think warrant further examination. This book invites you to look more closely at the different pieces of the mosaic, to turn them over and around, and to look at them in different lights and notice the colours, textures, and forms. We hope that it will engage you in bringing the pieces together in ways that work well for you and your communities.

This book is meant to foster a dialogue with and amongst readers. We offer up our ideas and reflections in search of a Social Capital Mosaic to prompt understanding and further dialogue so that those involved in communities can live and practice differently within them. Ask yourself questions, as we did in the writing of this book: "Where does this take me and my practice? What fits given my experience? What can I add to these ideas? How might I use these ideas? What will I do differently now?" We believe that a new understanding can come out of collective experience and reflections, which is critical for the ongoing evolution, understanding, and practical application of enhancing social capacity within communities.

We have designed this book around four parts. Part One presents the challenges that we, individually and collectively, encountered as we set about to make the world a better place for people. It also talks about how we understand these challenges and how they inhibit communities. Part Two speaks to the vision of community, healthy community, and a reformulation of social capital. Specifically, we identify the values, pieces of a Social Capital Mosaic, and a process for creating a Culture of Inquiry. In Part Three we present the pieces in a Social Capital Mosaic and how, in our experience, they reflect community values. Part Four explores how to start the process of creating a Social Capital Mosaic. Questions are posed for communities and community members that want to live in a different way.

Throughout the book we have interspersed stories which we think illustrate ideas to convey to readers. All of these stories are drawn from our practice and represent personal epiphanies.

Critical aspects of the literature on social capital are included in this book when they are similar to our Canadian experiences of enhancing community capacity. Singular ideas are not always credited to particular authors but all authors are credited in the bibliography for creating and being part of the larger discussion on enhancing social capacity.

When I was about 6 or 7, my dad was commissioned to design a number of very large mosaic murals. I recall looking through the many different sketches on his drafting table and the way in which he experimented with different themes and colour schemes. I was proud that my dad had so many beautiful ideas. The materials were then assembled to transform these sketches into living murals. I loved playing with the different glass pieces of the mosaic. I enjoyed the multitude of different colours and textures. I enjoyed watching the artisans as they deftly placed the different pieces –

Personal Story

each one beautiful in its own right.

For a long time, I only saw the pieces up close, but then I recall the experience of moving back from the mosaic and seeing the bigger picture for the first time. My dad's sketches — his vision — had taken form through the careful and artful placement of thousands of small pieces of glass.

This image of the mural and my experience of it coming to life fit so well with my experience of working on this book. I have been examining and experimenting with many different pieces of the mosaic, over many years. However, through the collective experience of writing I have taken steps outward and now see a bigger and grander picture.

Between the four of us we have one hundred years of experience in child, youth, family, and community work. Our journeys were separate but mutual. From our different positions within the community, voluntary, government, and private sectors we struggled daily with what we could do, should do, and might do. We were working within complex contexts and we knew that the challenges were greater than any one of us could handle on our own.

Each year at the University was like the last. Meetings entertained the same themes and the same issues. People spoke the same arguments and it was possible to predict who would speak next and what they would say. Those with the loudest voice or who represented the majority or who put forward the least intrusive solution got the most votes. However, winning or losing did not matter because people would go ahead and do what they wanted to do. The same memos crossed our desks, only the dates alerted us to the real change, it being another year. The same students showed up to class, the same classes were taught by the same instructors, and, once in awhile, we would take on an extraordinary committee as a way to enliven our work activities. Good grief — for an academy of higher education there was little learning happening here! Once in awhile someone would come along and try to tell you what to do, or what you ought to do, or what they were about to do. None of it mattered because we could affect nothing. All matters of consequence were dictated by the Faculty Handbook, or the memos, or the meetings which determined meaningless policy on matters such as the public display of pictures,

Frances' Story
"Is this working?"

or coffee rooms, or whether to call a part time faculty member a lecturer, a sessional, or part time instructor. It was time to leave. But would another place be any different?

So I went to a First Nations Child and Family Service organization, which was apprehending children at a high rate. On reserves, children were being lost — apprehended and sent to the city for foster care. The budget for the agency was seven million dollars and rising. Ideas on how to cope included hiring more workers and maintaining what they were doing to deal with the ever-increasing number of children who needed protection. Workers were untrained. Their personal lives were unhealthy. Workers arrived late to work, if they arrived at all. Smoke permeated the building and in some rooms it was difficult to see the other side of the room. There was no laughter; people did not greet each other in the halls, and workers kept to themselves. It was a never-ending story and it was not a fairytale! What could be done to rewrite the story?

Jennifer's Story
"What's happening here?"

I started on a journey towards a "better way" some 20 years ago. I thought I knew where I was going back then, or at least I thought I knew where I wanted to get to. The problem was that many of the paths that I tried took me to places that I didn't want to go to... so I skipped around a lot. I tried the child protection path, the community development path, the deinstitutionalization path. I also travelled to different territories and tried out the health promotion path and the social reform policy path. I trekked through the jungles of restructuring, reorganization, re-engineering, reform, devolution, and decentralization. I even took the path that joined the social, economic, environmental, and fiscal policy trails. On many occasions, I sensed the promise of something greater – something more inclusive, more systemic, more profound. On other occasions, I felt smothered by bureaucracy and overwhelmed by the negativity, powerlessness, and loss of spirit in the organizations and communities within which I lived and worked. I experienced episodes of great light and collective joy as well as deep darkness and isolation.

I realized that the problems facing our families, communities, and nations are too complex, the interdependencies too intricate, and the consequences of isolation and fragmentation too devastating for me to even think of travelling alone. Thinking and working alone, no matter what my level of power and authority, did not and could not work. And yet, even when working with others, we experienced great difficulty in affecting change within the broader systems. I sometimes now find myself reflecting with my colleagues and comrades... "Remember when...I really thought we were on to something there." I began to despair that so many wonderful ideas were not taking root in our communities.

A few years ago I was invited to be part of a team responsible for reforming child welfare. The team brought together an extraordinary concentration of talent and expertise, but we didn't seem to be able to produce anything of long term and positive significance. At the same time, I was part of another team that was not nearly as powerful, had little formal authority, and a short lived future. And yet, each day with this team was a joy. We did amazing work that was highly valued by our clients. We did this in the midst of a struggling and frequently dysfunctional larger system. In the end, both teams were disbanded. Afterwards, I went to Frances, who has been my mentor for almost 20 years,   and I asked... "What happened? How did this happen? What was the difference between the two teams? How can we work better together? How can I be part of making more of the good work happen?" Thus began the dialogue on Social Capital and our work together.

It was September of 1998 and I was seven years into an incredible journey of organizational transformation as the Executive Director of the Awasis Agency, a First Nation child and family services agency in the province of Manitoba. The Deputy Minister of the Department of Family Services and the Provincial Director of Child and Family Services travelled to Thompson to view our work. They invited me to work with them as a consultant to help reform the provincial child and family services system. The invitation was largely based on the success of the Awasis Agency in drastically reducing the number of children in care and in shifting its practice to a community wellness model.

I accepted the invitation and was granted the title of Provincial Director of Community Development. I was given the responsibility of promoting community involvement in the design and delivery of services. At first, I looked at the high number of aboriginal families impacted by the child and family services system, in particular the City of Winnipeg represented by Winnipeg Child and Family Services. Approximately 3,000 of Manitoba's children were in the care of

Gerard's Story
"What about the community?"

Winnipeg Child and Family Services. Approximately 70 per cent of these children were of aboriginal descent. This was especially alarming to the aboriginal community. The numbers translated into 30 aboriginal children in care per 1000 population, as compared to 1.6 per 1000 population for non-aboriginal children. Something was not working.

I began to spend time in the neighbourhoods and communities of Winnipeg and quickly discovered a diverse array of grassroots movements inclusive of aboriginal and non-aboriginal people. I learned that most, if not all, the services and programs that were perceived by the community as having a positive impact were community driven. In fact, there were hundreds of courageous people throughout the city working quietly, successfully and without public acclaim to battle social issues, reform schools, reclaim teens from gangs and drug abuse, and rebuild neighbourhoods. Yet I also learned that, to the formal system, these grassroots efforts were invisible, or if visible, dismissed as charismatic or inspiring but isolated anecdotes.

Some neighbourhoods and communities were engaged and experiencing success through transformation. Could their stories be told as a way to support other neighbourhoods and communities? Was there a way to use their stories to engage and build understanding in the formal system to inspire meaningful change? I decided to develop and publish a document in collaboration with the community to examine how local citizens in partnership with government can create Social Capital.

Much to my surprise, the department did not understand how it could engage in a joint writing project. One senior official commented that this could only raise the communities' expectations. It was at this point that I realized it may not be possible to reform the public child welfare system. I couldn't believe what he was saying. Why wouldn't we want to raise the expectations of communities? Doesn't raising expectations of communities prompt change that can promote healthier communities?

Through my years working as a counsellor in inner city schools and neighbourhoods, I became aware that the difficulties many children and families experienced were becoming more prevalent and complex in spite of the array of professional services available. Unemployment, inadequate housing, poverty, lack of vocational and educational training opportunities, and extreme social isolation permeated many families' daily experience.

As well, many students appeared to be disconnected from school life. This showed up in their lack of academic success and eventual school withdrawal. Our weekly student support meetings focussed on identifying and classifying students' learning and behaviour problems in order to plan our "interventions" and to secure more funding. The more evidence for the "at risk" nature of our students, the more funding we received. As a result, we became more problem-focused and crisis-driven.

However, despite our efforts, the issues that confronted families seemed to be expanding. Our reliance on counselling, as the primary approach of responding to students' concerns, maintained an individual family focus. This focus kept us from seeing communities and the resources within them.

The crisis orientation blinded us from recognizing the importance of promoting community belonging, capacity, and collective responsibility. How do I get out of these crises? What replaces them?

This Isn't Working

The first step in taking a different path is realizing that **this is not working**. The second step is to understand what is not working, why it is not working, and how we become part of it not working.

Thus began our journeys, with the realization that this wasn't working! It didn't work for us as individuals, for our organizations, for our communities, or our communities' families.

We noticed that, despite the "stuckness" experienced in our communities, there was no shortage of frenzied activity. We were part of this frenzied activity because we had bought into the dominant, professional, and "expert" driven service delivery model and system. We noticed that inherent to this service delivery system were values which contributed to our experience of "things not working." These values, defined in Figure 1, are perpetuated and indeed embraced by the service delivery system.

It doesn't work when there is...

These contribute to...

Objectification and Separation
- People treating each other as objects.
- People separating themselves from one another.

- mechanistic practices
- preoccupation with crisis and prophets offering quick fixes
- individualistic focus
- deficit/pathology orientation
- mistrust

Competition and Protectionism
People needing to win at others' expense, to feel safe.

- turfism
- power differentials that are reinforced through structures
- becoming outcome-driven
- distrust

Having and Knowing
People needing to have all the answers.

- deficit and pathology focus
- a preoccupation with knowing and "being right"
- an absence of learning despite the wealth of opportunities available
- being fear-driven
- incapacity to foster creativity and diffuse innovation

Control
People needing to control others through the use of power.

- program- and service-focussed and program- and service-driven systems
- rule-based and rule-driven systems
- bureaucratic hierarchies that reinforce power differentials
- firm attachment to the status quo
- inaccessibility of dominant governance structures

Simplification and Fragmentation
People wanting quick and easy solutions.

- lack of recognition for the dynamic and behavioural complexity of the challenges
- compartmentalization to make things easier to understand and work on
- fiscal or policy accountability taking priority over community and outcome accountability

Figure 1: Values That Do Not Work

Mechanistic Practices

We often refer to "systems" within our work — the child and family service system, the justice system, the education system, the income assistance system, the post-secondary system, and so on. We generally use these terms in reference to the array of benefits, services, and programs delivered under the auspices of one or another governance structure, typically government ministries. Sometimes we get courageous and talk about the "service delivery system" that is presumably a macro-system encompassing many of these other systems. However, in practice, we rarely act in a way that reflects a system's perspective, i.e. in appreciation of the many interconnections and interdependencies between the systems and subsystems.

Another frequently used term is "sector" — the community sector, the government sector, the voluntary sector, the private sector, and so on. This brings to mind images of wholes divided up into separate bits, such as a pie divided up into slices, a city divided into precincts, or a body defined by its distinct functions like respiration and digestion. While the notions of "systems" and "sectors" allow the opportunity to think in terms of relationships between the parts, it has been our experience that this type of thinking rarely happens.

We also find that labels are pervasive, and to this we add dichotomies. We are either clients or workers, union or management, professional or nonprofessional, government or non-government, public sector or private sector. Value perspectives are often attached to these dichotomies. One label is valued more highly than another, depending upon one's position and perspective. Labels also imply a power differential.

Objectification and Separation

Personal Story

A number of years ago, I was involved in a community and government partnership initiative that worked extremely well. It started out with two people — one a senior official from a government ministry and the other an agency executive director — believing that things could be different between the two sectors. Things had not been working for either sector at the time the partnership was formed. The government was under intense scrutiny and pressure to reform child, youth, family, and community services. The community sector, as the primary provider of service and thus the arms and legs of any reform effort, was suspicious of the government's intent and plans. These two people knew that this separation and polarization had to stop if there was to be any meaningful change in the "system."

Progress was slow. It took close to a year for the partnership to take root and for participants to come to believe that this was a genuine and valuable process. The participants began to learn from one another. They were less inclined to engage in wars over turf and special interests. They began to understand, appreciate, and then work with their interconnections and interdependencies. The "us and them" rhetoric was slowly being replaced with "we." Enthusiasm was spreading. Optimism was increasing.

Political direction changed and the partnership was terminated by government. Most of the government press releases sent out around this time stated government's commitment to partnership with community. The participants advocated for the partnership and came to be seen as agitators. According to the new powers, the problem was that the partnership that had been created wasn't the "right kind."

Individualism and Pathology

Working with individuals in isolation from their social context dominates our contemporary practice across all of the systems noted above. For example, there is a predominance of one-to-one work with clients, separation of children from families, defining communities as if homogeneous, "take charge" management, and reliance upon "quick fixes" to address problems and unilateral decision-making.

The individualistic perspective also connects to a deficit or pathology focus. Significant efforts are made to assess and diagnose the weaknesses of individuals in order to determine how to intervene. The presence and magnitude of the deficit or pathology is an indicator of that individual's status in life. This pathology perspective is what drives the delivery of benefits, services, and programs.

The long-standing emphasis on problem definition, as evident within social policy, assessment methods, professional language, and practice approaches has shaped our cultural tendency to see the world in individualistic terms. This focus has resulted in blaming the individuals, families, and communities for problems, deficits, and inadequacies.

Limited Solutions

In our experience, people usually work with two "solution boxes," one at each end of a continuum with little or no mainstream attention paid to the wide array of possibilities in between. Associated with the two-box model is a belief that there are causal relationships between phenomena. For example, in the youth justice area there has been heated debate on what should be done when young people commit "adult" acts of violence. People in Box One maintain that such youth should be punished as adults; adult acts equal adult consequences. Many contend that it is the very leniency of the *Young Offenders Act* and our youth justice system that perpetuates the cycle of violence amongst young people. If the system was more punitive, then youth wouldn't be as likely to act violently. By contrast, people in Box Two maintain that youth must be dealt with in an entirely different manner than adults, regardless of the seriousness of their crimes. They contend that the problems are social ones and an alternative humanistic and rehabilitative approach is necessary. If the system was more humanistic, then youth would rise above their social history and circumstances and become more responsible. Caught in the midst of the debates about responding in one way or another are the youth, families, and communities that are hurting.

In child protection in my province, we have two "solution boxes." Box One is the "apprehend" box. Box Two is the "keep with family" box. I have been around long enough to see the "child protection pendulum" swing back and forth between these two boxes three times. The swing seems to have been prompted by combinations of change in political leadership, public crises of faith and, increasingly, financial pressures. Crises have been prompted by alarming statistics or personal tragedies.

Each swing has created considerable confusion and turmoil in "the system." Under Box One, those disciplines/practitioners responsible for child protection are expected to remove children from their families when there is doubt about their continued safety. Children-in-care numbers increase. Under Box Two, these disciplines/ practitioners are expected to maintain the child in the family and, typically, offer a few predictable "support services" in an effort to keep the child "safe." Children-in-care numbers are maintained.

Personal Story

> Sometimes the practitioners get confused about the expectations and, in the eyes of the managers, "screw up" and make a "bad decision." This results in increased rules, accompanied by more prescribed procedures and scrutiny. Every so often a "prophet" comes along to suggest that "if only they did this...things would get better." Suddenly structures, tools, or other devices become the focus of attention.
>
> Isn't it interesting that we keep working with only two solution boxes? Isn't it strange that we keep looking to the prophets, rather than to ourselves, to provide the answers beyond this limited array of possibilities?

Often we hear the expression "there are many roads to Rome." As allied professions, very often we agree on the needs and even on the goals or vision, yet we spend countless hours arguing about how to get the job done. Our respective technologies are discipline-specific and we distrust technologies that we don't know or can't use. Perhaps, if we focussed on the needs, goals, and visions and trusted different ways to get the job done instead of being stuck in our boxes, we would spend less time arguing.

Competition and Protectionism

It's Just Turf

As social issues emerged so did the specialists. Each specialist group addressed some aspect of the larger social issue, resulting in the emergence of health specialists, welfare specialists, protection specialists, child and family specialists, finance specialists, legal specialists, and education specialists, to mention a few. Each speciality carved out a niche, bringing economic return to the specialists and clearly delineating and defining turf.

Specialists have designated their own turf and no one outside the speciality can, indeed must not, operate on another's turf (see Figure 2). These turfs are carefully protected through legislation and we pay dues to our professional associations to ensure that non-qualifying persons will be kept out. This evolution of professional groups represents the culture's obsession with individualism — a "top gun" approach to change motivated by winning, overcoming adversity, and looking good.

A closer look at Figure 2 reveals how defined turfs restrict all specialities in addressing the larger and more

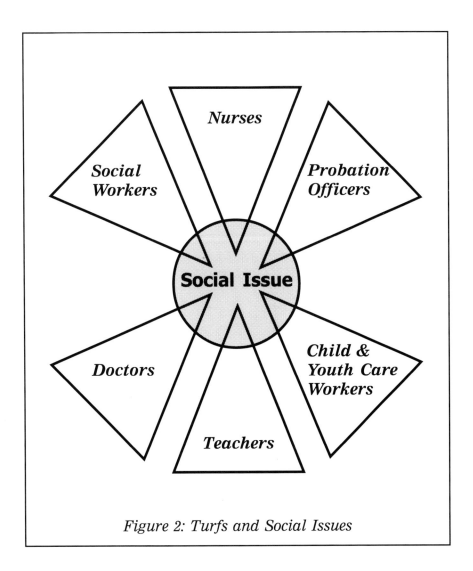

Figure 2: Turfs and Social Issues

complex social issues. Because each speciality or discipline looks at social issues and apparent solutions from its own professional perspective, there is no overall perspective of a social issue and limited ability to address any social issue. It seems obvious, however, that larger social issues require multiple perspectives, making all social issues, problems, and solutions beyond anyone's turf. Without an overall perspective of the social problem, no viable overall solutions can be generated.

Many communities today experience sickness or lack of health and wellbeing. Unhealthy communities are often communities that are isolated and have members that are isolated from each other. Because of this isolation, communities must struggle to get people involved as members take refuge in their homes, back yards, or the bush. Family members don't speak to each other. Grim-looking people walk around neighbourhoods neglecting to acknowledge others. Practitioners won't live in these communities, although their work environments may be equally unhealthy.

Within unhealthy work communities basic civilities are missing. Greetings are not extended, people are too busy for each other during coffee breaks, lunch is always on the fly, and primary conversational exchanges are hostile, critical, or full of gossip. Hate messages get left on the desks of sexual minority members. Misunderstood motivations and communications lead to competition, distancing, hatred, or even murder. Larger and larger numbers of people take sick leave as a means of escape.

Having and Knowing are Learning Disabilities

Knowing is Disabling

There is a pervasive learning disability within our defined specialities and their respective turfs. The disability is perpetuated through our fixation on having knowledge and knowing, which makes us confront learning opportunities with fear rather than wonder. Many of us derive our sense of self and belonging from having knowledge and knowing, as opposed to learning, creating, and doing. Indeed, we are expected to have and know, and we are rewarded for having and knowing. This orientation doesn't stop with individuals. Teams, groups, agencies, organizations, and communities are all vulnerable to this learning disability.

Because of this disability, we define problems as *problems* rather than challenges or opportunities. We criticize before we seek to understand. We look for something or someone to blame rather than seek the wisdom of others to rethink the problem. We persist in fragmentation and piecemeal analysis as the world becomes more and more interconnected. We valiantly wrestle these problems into the discipline-based solution boxes that we already know rather than create new boxes. We create problem-controlling bureaucracies when we say we want visionary enterprises.

The Perpetuation of Having and Knowing

How do we get to be in a place of having and knowing? Our social orientation to having and knowing relates closely to the way in which we have been educated. As students (rather than learners), we have been expected to "know" certain information and "have" certain skills as prescribed by the curriculum developers. Further, our dominant model of governance — hierarchical bureaucracies — perpetuates the having and knowing orientation. Bureaucracies are designed in the apparent interests of efficiency and effectiveness. People are recruited and assigned responsibility to perform on the basis of what they are assumed to know or have. They are given particular jobs or tasks and are expected to perform them according to a particular standard. The dominant rules for people working within bureaucracies are:

- remain in control
- maximize "winning" and minimize "losing"
- suppress negative feelings, and
- be rational.

The purpose of these rules is to avoid embarrassment, threat, or loss and to avoid feeling vulnerable or incompetent.

To illustrate how having and knowing operates we offer several examples for your consideration. Imagine that you know about a good playground for your children. This knowledge supports you in finding a pleasant place to spend some leisure time with your kids. You know about a resource in your community. Now imagine what would happen if you moved to a different neighbourhood, or if the playground became unsafe, or if the type of equipment was no longer suitable for your children. Imagine if you didn't seek an alternative. Perhaps you would lament the loss of the old playground or of how your children used the playground. Perhaps you would keep going there despite its inadequacy. You still have your "knowing" about the playground, but there was no learning about alternatives. You stay wedded to history, location, or practices that no longer meet your needs or your children's needs.

As an organizational example, imagine that you are the coordinator for a parenting program. You have a lot of knowledge about parenting skills and child development and have developed a program of which you are very proud. You have offered this program for over five years and government workers happily provide you with more referrals than you can handle. But lately you've noticed that the parents are different; they aren't participating in the way that they used to. They are struggling with different issues and having a harder time staying with the eight week program. You "know" that you have a good program, based on evaluation research. You "know" it has worked before and that there is nothing wrong with the program. Perhaps you conclude that the problem lies with the participants; they just aren't motivated enough to make a difference in their lives. Perhaps the problem lies with the referral process; the workers are just sending you people indiscriminately. Perhaps the problem lies with government policies; after all, if they hadn't changed the welfare eligibility policies, the participants wouldn't have to spend as much time seeking work or being preoccupied with financial concerns.

When you come from a "place of knowing" you seek to find the source of the problems "out there" and "with them." You may lament the passing of the old days and old ways that were both familiar and positive. You may feel anger and frustration that those "out there" are making things more difficult for you. You may "take action" and set out stricter guidelines for referrals. You may go to office meetings and explain the purpose of your program and identify the types of clients that should be referred to your program. You may do nothing; after all, the problem lies not with the program and delivery but with things that are "beyond your control" (i.e., the characteristics and attitudes of participants, the referring workers, or the system). Perhaps you may think that, as long as the funding keeps coming for what you are doing, you need not worry.

Many of the organizations and communities — no matter how small — within which we work, reflect the bureaucratic model. The dominant expectation is that we will know how to do our job. Even if circumstances change, it is assumed that only minor tinkering in our knowing will be necessary in order to regain our capacity for peak efficiency.

> I was involved in a major restructuring initiative within a large organization. "Parts" from a number of other organizations were being amalgamated into one larger organization. It was assumed that the people coming together would simply continue to practice what they "knew" within their former organizations. Therefore, there was no perceived need for people to "learn" anything other than where they fit within the new organizational structure and, thus, who they would be accountable to, how to use the computer systems and what the rules were around certain types of practices such as information sharing. The organizational bureaucracy assumed that people would need just a little additional information and some technical training in order to make the transition from where they were to where they were now expected to be. At the same time, this restructuring effort was supposed to "'fundamentally transform the system!"

How often have you heard these words? "Susan is our computer expert" or "Charan knows about the Indo-Canadian community" or "we need to find an accountant to sit on the Board so that they can take care of all the financial stuff" or "we need someone on welfare to sit on this committee to represent the interests of the poor." Susan, Charan, the accountant, and the person receiving income assistance undoubtedly have a great deal of expertise and experience to share, and their perspective is important to the process. However, there are risks in this approach.

Individual risk: *Not knowing* is seen to be a weakness. When people are *expected* to know the answer, they may come to believe that they do indeed know. If they are aware that they don't know, they take great efforts to ensure that others do not discover their "weaknesses." Once people share what they know, they are finished. They believe they have no other contribution to make. People shut down to the possibility of doing things differently and may operate from a place of confusion and fear. They operate from confusion when things don't work the way that they are supposed to and from fear of being "found out." When people are faced with complex problems, and what they know doesn't work, they are fearful of being blamed for their lack of knowing the answer. Therefore, they seek to locate the source of the problem outside of themselves and struggle to keep intact their old ways of knowing. A pattern of "defensive reasoning" sets in.

Group risk: Groups that are expected to know or have the answer respond in a similar way to the individual. Many disciplines or professions are assumed to, or profess to, know all there is to know about a particular subject or area of practice. Thus they become impervious to learning opportunities. Similarly, hierarchical organizations are comprised of groups that are assumed to be the experts in particular practice areas (e.g., the human resource branch, the child protection team, the public health branch, the youth justice division, the family services team). When the individuals within the group close down their minds to alternatives and options, the group loses access to their diverse perspectives, experiences, and creative capacities. The group's ability to respond to changing circumstances is seriously disabled because the group perceives a risk in going outside their turf to find the answers. They fear that their group will be perceived in a bad light for not having all the answers.

Organizational and Community risk: In a system where individuals (typically those from a particular discipline or holding a particular position of authority) are expected to know or have the answers, members of the community give up their power to these experts. The risk to the community is that its members' perspectives on the problems are rarely expressed, let alone acknowledged. The strengths and capacity inherent in the community are overshadowed by the deficit or pathology focus of the experts, and the complex issues facing the community continue to be forced into the same old solution boxes.

Characteristics of Having and Knowing

The dominant frame of mind with having and knowing is one of pessimism and competitiveness. For example, there is a belief that people need to have rules to follow, otherwise they won't know how to behave correctly. The rules result in a perspective that there is, in fact, little choice about how things are done. It is presumed that either the rules, or the people who make the rules, will call the shots. The objective becomes "follow the rules" or "avoid being consequenced for not following the rules." This sets up a situation in which people blame each other, or groups blame other groups, for messes that arise when either the rules aren't followed or the rules (and the policies and programs) don't work.

People do not work collaboratively within the having/ knowing orientation. The "top dogs," experts, and prophets are given considerable power and authority and the rest are seen as tools for getting the job done. Outliers, eccentrics, and renegades are quickly censored or fired as "bad apples" and are often held up as a warning to others to control their behaviour and follow the rules. Therefore, people tend to keep their heads down and hope that each successive wave of controversy and challenge rolls over them quickly. People "park themselves" at the door of their work; there is no point in bringing themselves and their experiences, ideas, and perspectives into the room.

Within this orientation "learning" is framed as training or education. The emphasis is placed on formal training events to ensure people adequately implement new procedures or learn specific skills or techniques.

Governance as Social Control

Any form of governance is represented by a social system or network of people. The system generates its own form of governance by defining its patterns of interaction, structure, and rules and its regulations, policies, procedures, and norms. Governance is a form of social control.

The prevailing form of governance in Canada is grounded in the Westminster model of hierarchical bureaucracies. Under this model, it was assumed that the masses needed to be directed by the aristocracy, who were more educated and more capable. As it was assumed that membership in this elite group was preordained, it was believed that the aristocracy knew best and the masses should be both grateful and compliant. This history has created and perpetuated hierarchical bureaucratic systems.

Any form of governance is controlling because it provides a structure that is based on principles. These principles are the foundation for the rules and procedures that guide members in the community. The rules and procedures represent the larger system within which other organizations operate and our daily lives are lived. The rules and procedures become the focus of what we do and how we operate. As such, governance touches our lives on a daily basis; governance determines the rules about who participates and how with regards to health, education, welfare, business, and so on.

> The Indian Act dictated that First Nations people live on reservations. This kind of legislation limited First Nations people in location which ultimately affected other aspects of their lives such as control, class, privilege, and influence. Currently, school legislation dictates who can attend which schools. Again, limiting location affects control, class, privilege and influence. Some universities get upset when universities from other provinces invade their jurisdiction. However, doesn't it make sense that students are in the best position to know with whom they wish to study? Should students not have the opportunity to work with certain scholars who certainly are available in these times through advanced technologies no matter where they live? Such examples show that parameters or rules about what certain people can and cannot do limit people's capacity for being involved in and doing other things.

The overall effects of governance are far-reaching in terms of what and how things can be done; participants, the nature of their participation, and the subsequent benefits of participation are influenced. The individual's capacity is limited by the potential inherent in the individual and the context that surrounds the individual within that particular governance. These pre-existing endowments embedded in governance structures clearly set the stage for playing out our lives. In many instances, it is the luck of the draw that positions the individual within a governance structure, and the influence of that structure dictates opportunities for personal growth and development for the rest of one's life.

How Bad Is It?

Many levels of governance have been created. There are elected municipal, band, tribal, district, regional, provincial, and federal levels of governance, as well as various voluntary and appointed governance structures. At all levels, many governance structures have evolved into huge bureaucracies. Most of our Canadian organizations and institutions are modelled on the bureaucratic model in an attempt to be efficient and effective. Yet in recent times such structures are failing to produce results that justify their levels of spending.

Because they are embedded in these bureaucracies social, health, justice, and educational programs stand apart from the social fabric. Such programs seem to be suspended, as if in space, rather than within and related to the members of a community. Individual members in bureaucratic systems often have only one thing in common, such as their focus on an illness, a geographic location, or an age group and, therefore, do not represent a true community, never mind having a sense of being *in* community.

"I'd like all the teams in this place to operate like yours," my CEO tells me. "Your team has the big picture in mind and yet you really listen to what your clients (regional service providers) need and figure out ways to take care of the details that matter to them. I really like your spirit and your creativity. You guys have been a lot of fun to work with. But..." he continues and I begin to tense up in anticipation of what the "but" will mean for us. "But you know we have to cut back and consolidate. I have to let those guys in the field sink or swim now. There isn't really a place for your team any more. We've gone through the big change. We're through the stuff that you guys were so good at." I think he means the "stuff" of relationship-building, of supporting, of bringing people together to make something new happen. "It's time to hunker down and get on with the business of delivering the programs. We'd like you to stay on — you're a good leader. Of course, we'll do our best to find places for all your staff."

I stop listening to him and the internal discussion takes over. "We are too far out there for this place. We broke too many rules. How dare he think that there's no need for more change, for more creativity, for more support — we're just getting started, we need to do so much more! I'm not a good leader in isolation from the people who matter to me and from the issues that drive me." The feelings flood over me — the sense of impending loss. I'd never worked with a more dynamic, energized, talented, and creative team. Every member had many gifts, and, in this team, they freely shared them. Collectively we were amazing. In facing the demise of our team — in the name of bureaucratic consolidation and efficiency — I imagined myself having to trade the open fields that we had collectively explored for a closed train car that hurtled down the tracks to the same old blackened rail yards that we'd been going to for decades.

The bureaucratic reality is actually taking a turn for the worse. In our experience of current bureaucratic systems, members of the organization are constrained by a need to have and control, a need to be efficient through simple solutions and the norms, rules, policies, and procedures that bring about separation and competition. There is no creativity in finding solutions — only questioning as to what the rules and policies are rather than questioning what *could* be done. Following the rules actually aborts formulation of the issues and judicious consideration of alternative and innovative solutions.

The norms, rules, policies, and procedures define the parameters of programs by dictating the structure and ways of operating. Such constraints affect the resources, daily operations, and outputs of programs. Even worse, these constraints are determined centrally by elected and designated officials and not by the people who must operate within them. For example, workers such as child and youth care workers, social workers, managers, nurses, and teachers, are hired into bureaucratic organizations where there are existing mandates, mission statements, and visions. These newly hired personnel arrive to fulfil the mandate, mission, or vision as prescribed by others. Their roles are defined in job descriptions. The resources are allocated according to some policy, rule, or guideline. Workers are monitored to ensure that they not only play inside the box but play by the rules inside the box! If one does not play by the rules, someone will come along to "correct" the problem and get the person on board with the rest of the team! This monitoring not only ensures compliance, it engenders "looking over the shoulder" to see who may be watching.

Personal Story

I'm working with an organization that delivers benefits to people with disabilities. In the course of a team meeting that I attended, the new supervisor announced that he wanted to redesign the waiting area to be more accessible and comfortable for the many clients with mobility impairments. As many clients are served at wickets in the front office, he wanted to lower the counter for one wicket to allow people to sit down while being assisted by the staff. Several staff interjected that this was a bad idea. The clients would have an easier time reaching over the counter to "get at" the workers. This had happened once, they said, and they didn't want it to happen again. The comments and criticisms of this and other ideas continued. I picked up on their fear. I sensed that they felt under siege. I sensed their "stuckness" — their inability to see things in any other way than negatively. They seemed to be saying "Keep the barriers up. It's us against them."

Indeed, there had been such a "critical incident" in this office. As I understand it, a very confused, exasperated, and desperate client climbed over the counter and grabbed the worker's shirt while saying "For God's sake, look at me! Listen to me!" In the end, a young man could not have his needs acknowledged or addressed and faced criminal charges. A worker was upset and frightened. An office became protective and defensive, and a system became even more unresponsive to this worker and other clients.

Bureaucracies have taken a bad turn by moving away from efficiently responding to public needs, and moving towards accountability only to their own existing policies, procedures, and legislation. This focus on policy accountability involves constant questioning of what people are doing and whether they are doing it according to the rules. Bureaucrats get preoccupied with developing systems to monitor and control. Thinking is discouraged; doing what is expected is all that matters.

In these bureaucracies people operate as if there is a control centre. In it exists an ultimate authority by the name of "Pal," which has a mind of its own. In reporting to the elusive Pal, people make decisions in an "as if world" which is not only removed from people and neighbourhoods, but has a separate agenda of control to its own end. This agenda brings with it a perception of being the boss of others, of having success and status, and of larger salaries accompanied by their respective titles. For example, we know of some alarming profile data of senior administrators in a provincial government. The administrative profile is: high in dominance ("Get out of my way. I am responsible for everything."), high in structure ("I like the routines and deal with crises through the application of routines."), and low on interpersonal skills ("It is easier to be a lone wolf than to work within a larger team."). Perhaps these administrators have become our Pals!

Personal Story

This senior group of bureaucrats were a happy lot. With their many years of bureaucratic experience, they moved from position to position taking turns hiring each other and keeping each other out of harm's way. The problems kept growing, but little substantive change happened in their worlds. They were good at finding reasons for why things were tough "out there." Every Friday afternoon the office all but closed as the boys held "meetings" at the bar from 2:00 pm on.

They knew that there was some risk in bringing a new person into this culture. After all, a new person might not play by the rules and, worse yet, might find them out. Not to worry, they concluded. No one had been in this business as long as they had, and no one would dare to blow the whistle. Even if they did, who would believe such an outrageous accusation?

No Accountability

Over the past 30 years, the focus in government has been on "getting things under control" — control of policy, control of money, damage control. Generations of administrators have been selected to get things under control, and these administrators continue to select people who continue to select people to get things under control. Of course, the control over the many aspects of services is rarely coordinated, resulting in fragmentation rather than collaboration and integration. One ministry may be responsible for designing programs in light of their mandate, and a completely separate ministry may rule on the amount of money available for the programs.

Usually programs are accountable fiscally. They are also accountable to the public perception of a program, or the public perception of the politician responsible for a program. Accountability is generally unrelated to other aspects of the program, resulting in high level managers making short-term decisions that have nothing to do with the mandate of the program but everything to do with controlling the spending. For example, when there is political pressure to "protect the children," spending is not tightly monitored. What is important is to protect the children so that politicians don't look bad — to take any child into care if there is any doubt about their need for protection. When the money runs out near the end of the fiscal year, it is decided to take children into care only when it is absolutely necessary. Clearly neither decision is related to the mandate or the objectives of the child protection program.

No Reflection, Choice, or Discretion
The above example points out the long-standing illusion within bureaucracies that reflection and choice exist. In fact, there is little time for reflection as people in the system are busy focussing on understanding and complying to the rules. **Reflections are limited to those options that are already bound by the parameters and limitations of the defined policy, procedures, and legislation.** Thus, choices are also limited.

Choices are limited not necessarily by the policies themselves but by the rules that emerge through the translation of the policy in practice. Policy makers set the expectations when they write the policy. Policy implementers, presuming that there is little or no room for discretion, translate the policy and entrench it in rules for operating. These become the rules in use regardless of the original intent of the policy.

Not surprisingly, the lack of room left for reflection, choice, and discretion fosters great debate on matters of little importance. Should this word or that word be used in delineating policy and procedures? Who should be allowed to use the coffee room? Who gets which parking space?

We have observed that many workers, who have been bound up in hierarchical bureaucracies, are extremely uncomfortable with open space. Even when legislation, policies, and procedures allow them to exercise considerable discretion, they want to create rules. We have found numerous examples of "office rules" or "rules of thumb" that people have created and entrenched in order to deal with ambiguity and limit their responsibility for exercising professional discretion and judgment. Newcomers or outsiders to the office are frequently told "This is the way things are done here. It's the only way." Dialogue and reflection never get off the ground.

Another example that exposes the weakness of the traditional bureaucratic model relates to labour/union strife and conflict. In the absence of trust, shared goals, and collective purpose, there is mistrust, competition, and rule-boundedness. Co-creation, synergy, and interdependence are not a real option because whatever might be created synergistically or interdependently would

Personal Story

likely violate the existing norms, rules, and procedures. In addition, there is little room for relationships that require trust and creativity because there is no need for creativity. There is only room for compliance.

No Good News

We noticed many other characteristics of contemporary, hierarchical bureaucracies:

- Bureaucracies have an "us and them" orientation whether it is between clients and staff, headquarters and regions, community and government, etc. This creates separation and distance. "We do it better than they do."
- Bureaucracies lack the personal touch. There is little or no attention paid to individuals and their needs, relationships, potential and capacity. "I don't matter – nothing matters."
- Bureaucracies are fragmented and operate within discrete units, including programs and services, events and responses. "We can't help you – it's not our department."
- Bureaucracies are competitive, self-serving, and self-protective. "We won't work in multidisciplinary teams – everyone knows that some disciplines aren't qualified."
- Bureaucracies use reductionistic causality which results in simple thinking and simple solutions. "If this...then this..."
- Bureaucracies take away choice, thus destroying spirit, motivation, commitment, learning, and creativity. "Why bother? No one cares."

Simplification and Fragmentation

Understanding Complexity – "I really don't know, and it's worse than I thought!"

Because of the complexity of social challenges, managers and decision-makers face increasingly difficult challenges as either dynamic complexity or behavioural complexity increases. **Dynamic complexity** addresses the extent to which actions and outcomes can be linked, observed, and understood. Where actions can be easily linked to outcomes, dynamic complexity is low. Dynamic complexity escalates, however, when the connections between actions and outcomes are not well understood or when certain actions lead to a variety of short and long term, intended and unintended consequences.

Behavioural complexity addresses the extent to which there is diversity in the aspirations, mental models, and even values and basic assumptions of decision-makers. High behavioural complexity is characterized by deep conflict in assumptions, beliefs, and perspectives, which can occur when there are community members representing different genders, races, ethnicity, etc. Where there is high behavioural complexity, it is difficult to get people to agree on what should be done because they see the world very differently and because they have different agendas or goals. This is evidenced through different movements which have rocked many organizations (i.e., equity initiatives involving race, gender, and ethnicity).

When both dynamic and behavioural complexity are high, the challenges can be overwhelming. This is especially so because the types of skills required may diverge. Dynamic complexity requires high level conceptual and systems thinking skills; behavioural complexity requires high level interpersonal and facilitative skills.

When dynamic complexity is high, management interventions tend, at best, to improve matters in the short term, only to create more problems in the long term. Even worse, many of the most pressing problems people face are actually the unintended consequences of past "solutions." For example, welfare was intended to support people to get back on their feet. However, it created its own industry which in the long run has fostered dependency.

In contrast, low dynamic complexity occurs in situations where it is easier to link actions with outcomes. When a supervisor working with pay clerks, for example, changes the order in which tasks are performed for the bi-weekly pay schedules, it is generally possible to directly observe the impact of those changes on processing efficiency.

We know that decision-makers have great difficulty learning from experience in the face of dynamic complexity. During a series of experimental studies, decision-makers took actions that were ineffective. When subsequently presented with the same or similar challenges, the effectiveness of their actions did not improve based on what they had learned in the previous trial. In other words, they didn't learn from their experience!

Sometimes, when an organization perceives itself as having a problem, it is almost too easy to blame the problem on something that does not require too much soul searching. Ineffective communication is a favourite. Research into dynamic complexity suggests that it is not adequate to simply get people to communicate more effectively because the problem is not communication. The problem is that our cognitive maps are much simpler than the real life systems we routinely encounter.

Tame, Wicked and Messy
We have identified four types of challenges: tame, wicked, messes, and wicked messes. These are outlined in the following matrix.

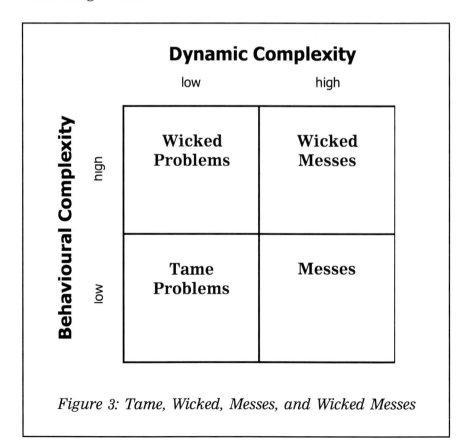

Figure 3: Tame, Wicked, Messes, and Wicked Messes

When problems of low dynamic complexity combine with problems of low behavioural complexity, the result is a "tame problem." Tame problems can be solved using conventional analytic methods involving data collection and static analysis (i.e., analysis that does not require dealing with delays, multiple feedback loops, and nonlinear relationships). Tame problems can be solved in isolation. Traditionally, tame problems are broken down into parts that can be solved independently by different groups of people. Solutions to different parts of larger problems can then be integrated into an overall solution because (1) there are no significant dynamic interconnections between the parts and (2) different actors share common values and goals. We don't see many of these any more!

"Wicked problems" are those where behavioural complexity is high, where complex underlying social realities are inescapable, and where different groups of key decision-makers hold assumptions, values, and beliefs which are in opposition to one another. Geertz (1973) describes the "loss of orientation" that arises in the absence of an overriding social theory or ethic. When there is no overriding social theory and ethic, people see the situation from their different perspectives and value bases. They propose strategies in terms of how they see it. Moreover, the fundamental differences in values remain in the background and are typically "undiscussable." "Wickedness," according to King (1993), "occurs when people confer immutability on value assumptions and ideological considerations." We see a lot of these situations!

"Messes" arise when dynamic complexity is high. These are puzzles that are not so much "solved" as sorted out in terms of their inherent complexities. Messes cannot be solved by solving component problems in isolation from one another because there are significant couplings between isolated problem symptoms. For example, the breakdown of discipline in the classroom cannot be addressed effectively by stricter teacher control because the larger parenting and community systems from which the students come have also broken down. Sorting out messes is complicated by "vicious and virtuous cycles," "tragedies of the commons," "shifting the burden," and similar dynamics which are often neglected by individual decision-makers under pressure to "fix" problems quickly.

This discussion is important for three reasons. First, dynamic and behavioural complexity characterize the most vexing social problems, both within organizations and within society. Examples of this include global environmental problems, government deficits, erosion of public education, racism and disenfranchisement of whole sub-populations, poverty, and community breakdown. Secondly, such problems go largely unrecognized for what they are — complex, interconnected social problems. There is a tendency to treat such problems as if they had either purely technical solutions or purely behavioural solutions and as if the key were to simply gather the right data and analyse it correctly, get people communicating more effectively, offer the right rehabilitative programs, or elect the right official. Lastly, theory, tools, and methods for addressing such problems are largely underdeveloped. We see this as our challenge!

It's Just a Wicked Mess!

We are challenged by numerous wicked messes. Wicked messes, where both dynamic and behavioural complexity are high, include taxation, First Nations land claims and governance, poverty and welfare, child protection, environmental degradation and depletion of natural resources, loss of traditional industries and economic means in communities, aging of population and elder care, mental health, education, escalation of violence in communities, withdrawal of people into protective enclaves, and diminished community activity.

Wicked messes have become the focus of attention in our various sectors and systems and that responses to these messes have been quite predictable: simple quick fixes to manage them; competition between the various disciplines or sectors to profess the answer; and, pulling away from the mess and attributing the responsibility to others to fix it. The mess has been objectified and separated from its context. The various sectors and systems have endeavoured to control the mess and all those associated with it.

Our approach to wicked messes assumes that new syntheses of previously disconnected approaches will be required, along with new theory and methods. Effective syntheses entail a blending of "technical" and "behavioural" approaches. Conceptual and analytic tools are required to understand complex dynamics, along with the thinking and inquiry skills needed to reveal and suspend long-held beliefs, values, and assumptions.

Supporting the entire effort is a recognition of the complexity and the newness of the territory and a belief in the power of a community working together. Unless we learn to learn from and with one another across traditional organizational, cultural, disciplinary and professional boundaries, real progress is not possible.

In the face of these kinds of messes and our realization that our traditional ways of responding cannot work, the four of us are committed to finding new ways to address the messes. We share this commitment with many others in our communities. To find direction and new ways of thinking, we looked to our own experiences and the social capital literature. From reviewing successes, we discovered that some community members lived different lives than those lived in many communities. Further, to handle the complexities of communities and their issues, we found that a much broader and more comprehensive mosaic of social capital concepts was needed.

Finally, we suggest that because of the different values, the larger perspective of community, and the pieces of the mosaic, community members need a different process of relating and working together. We think our discoveries offer the potential for creating different realities in our communities.

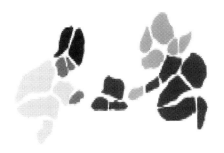

Part 2

Rethinking Community and Social Capital

It is in communities that people struggle with problems that are **tame, wicked, messes, and wicked messes**. Some contemporary wicked messes include:

- taxation
- First Nations land claims and governance
- welfare
- child protection
- environmental degradation and depletion of natural resources
- loss of traditional industries and economic means in many communities
- aging of population and elder care
- mental health
- education
- escalation of violence in our communities, withdrawal of people into protective enclaves, and diminished community activity

At the same time, we find it intriguing that most people with whom we have lived and worked want the same things that we do. We have worked within some of the poorest and wealthiest communities in this country. No matter what type of community, people want:

- a safe community
- a good place to raise their kids
- meaningful educational and work opportunities

- decent and affordable housing
- access to health supporting opportunities — nutritious food; good health care; exercise, recreation and leisure
- green spaces and beautiful environments
- just, fair, and accessible systems of governance
- equality, freedom, and personal options
- connections with others

In our experience, the things that people want have not, and cannot be, produced, by traditional social programs and services. What is wanted cannot be produced when the focus is on the messes rather than on the context for the messes. What is the context for messes? **The context is the community**. What people are saying is they want healthy communities in which to raise their families, be connected with others, work together, and achieve their dreams and aspirations. Community is the context within which we all hope to live a life of health and wellbeing.

What is Community?

We need to have some mutual understanding of what is meant when talking about community. For us, community is simply a collection of relationships. Therefore, community can be placed geographically (e.g., in Winnipeg), or institutionally or organizationally (e.g., The University of Victoria School of Child and Youth Care or The Awasis Agency). Community can also be defined in a unique manner that captures the relational nature of the members or participants in the community (e.g., the community of scholars at the university or the community of teens who are part of a local gang). In terms of neighbourhoods, community can be defined as the "community north of the river," or "the school in the community north of the river," or "the parents of the community school north of the river." Work organizations, due to their being a collection of people who have a relationship through their work, are also communities, as are the subsections within organizations .

By defining community as a collection of relationships, it can be inferred that, **more important than the designated space or location of the community is the relational nature of community members**. Those who have a sense of community and live and work in community have some identification with their community. They feel like they belong to that community and share mutual caring for each other. Within some communities, family and community are one and the same. Community members make no distinction between their relationships with their family members and their relationships with the rest of the community.

We started out in our respective practices working with individuals. While we were either trained or moved to work with individuals in the context of their families or significant relationships, we initially left the bigger picture alone. After all, what would we do about poverty, racism, historical inequities, and abuses? We practised in community settings, but we weren't necessarily _of_ the community. Nor were we necessarily guided and directed by the community. In fact, we were more frequently directed by the bureaucracies that we either worked for or were funded by! There came a time for each of us when we realized that this wasn't good enough.

The image comes to mind of the caring person downstream of the waterfall, who has taken on the job of pulling out from the water the souls who have fallen over the waterfall. Day in and day out, she pulls people out. The numbers grow and the speed with which they come down the river increases. Finally — weary and overwhelmed — she gives up. As she rests on the bank of the river, she reflects on her years of pulling people out and questions, "Why are so many people falling over the edge of the waterfall?"

Personal Story

When community members characterize the environment they want to be a part of, what they describe goes beyond community to **healthy community**. Because there can be uncertainty over the definition of a healthy community, building a healthy community becomes a complex matter.

We propose that healthy community is an idea of how community members want their community to be. Healthy community is the shared vision of what it means to be healthy within community. The healthy community is based on the values of the community as represented in Figure 4.

As noted earlier, many communities want the same thing. They want communities that are good, safe places to raise kids, that offer meaningful educational and work opportunities, that have decent and affordable housing, that provide access to health-supporting opportunities, green spaces, and beautiful environments, that ensure just and

Healthy Community is the Goal

Ideas of Healthy Community

Information/Facts **+** *Values*

Figure 4: Ideas of Healthy Community

accessible systems of governance, that promote equality, freedom, personal options, and connections with others.

Creating healthy communities may require a philosophical inquiry about what it takes to build health and to promote the living of healthier lives. Thinking in terms of health puts the focus on a strengths orientation. The central assumption of the strengths orientation is that people and communities have inherent strengths, resources, talents, and possibilities for growth. This orientation takes a broader ecological perspective and, in an attempt to redress inequities, addresses social, political, and economic barriers to community opportunities. Joe Flower's (1994) vision of a healthy community from this perspective is probably one of the best:

> ...safer lives in stronger families with less stress, better nutrition, more information and greater wisdom...are the same things we can do to help make a community more democratic, wealthier, more interconnected, better educated, and even happier. You can't build healthy individuals in a sick community.

Creating a shared vision of health within community can be problematic in communities that have experienced generations of dysfunction and lack of health. In these communities, the absence of health and the predominance of unhealthy lifestyles have become the norm. When unhealthy lifestyles become the norm, they are viewed as "acceptable," "good enough," or even "healthy." They become the norm that is used to generate information, facts, and values for the vision. It is important to view this confusion between the norm and healthy as an opportunity for the community to learn together.

Community health research may offer some evidence of health facts as may public information on different aspects of health and wellbeing. The community must share information and perspectives on "unhealthy" and "healthy" and learn together to create a vision of healthy community. Some health indicators to consider are suggested below.

Economic Health: The ability of individuals to meet their basic economic needs; the amount of economic opportunity that exists for employment; and the opportunity for education, job training, supervision, etc. that would enable personal and job advancement.

Physical Health: The availability of health promotion, prevention, and treatment opportunities and services that meet the medical needs of individuals; the availability of nutritious food, safe water and housing; and the opportunities for healthy lifestyle activities.

Social Health: The level of social capacity inherent in individuals and community as defined by strong reciprocal relational ties. Social health is manifest in social, recreational, and community-based activities that bring people together in laughter, fun, and goodwill towards each other.

Emotional Health: The availability of support services, learning and personal development opportunities; the degree of strong relationships; a sense of control over one's own life; and the ability to have an effect at various levels of community (i.e., individual, family, and community).

Personal Story

Recently we have been a part of a shift in child, youth, and family services from the more traditional client-centred practice or approach towards community-centred approaches. In addition, we have observed the implementation of health transfer agreements for First Nations communities. In both cases, for the most part, this has been about transplanting the traditional services into a community frame and disregarding community interests or desires.

A New Reality in Community

Our experience convinces us that people are pretty clear about the kind of communities they want. They have a vision of community which reflects values such as safe, meaningful, decent, affordable, healthy, green, fair, equitable, free, and connectedness.

To achieve this generic vision of healthy community — this new reality — the community must be the designer of their Social Capital Mosaic. This requires a new way of thinking about the community. We propose that there are three critical aspects of community to rethink. First, there are community values which are the foundation for a different way of being. Secondly, there are the different pieces of a Social Capital Mosaic that reflect the implementation of values in the community. In addition, there is a different process which we call a Culture of Inquiry. In the Culture of Inquiry, community members operate in a different way to design their Social Capital Mosaic.

Building this reality requires living and thriving within a different reality from that which is usually experienced within community organizations and neighbourhoods. This reality represents a shift from "community control" to "community enhancement." The "community control" and "community enhancement" positions are distinguished by fundamental value differences about what is important and what is not, and how things should or should not be.

Keep in mind that visions are pictures of what is possible and what we strive to achieve. Visions are often influenced by what we know and what surrounds us, and can sometimes be limiting. For some people, the vision is to have success, control, influence, and knowledge that will benefit me, the individual, and my achievements. For others, the vision is about being in relationships, learning, working

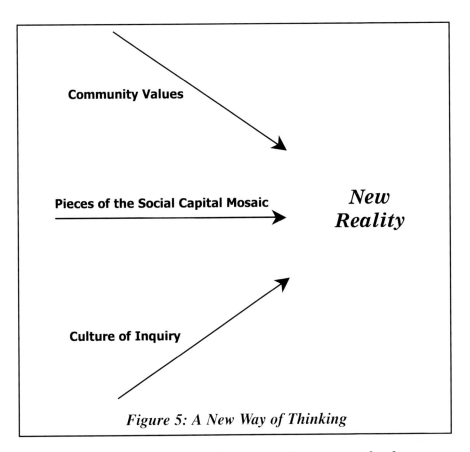

Community Values

Pieces of the Social Capital Mosaic

New Reality

Culture of Inquiry

Figure 5: A New Way of Thinking

together toward common objectives that serve the larger community and the common good — a vision of living together in harmony.

These kinds of value differences account for why things happen and why they do not. They determine what can be done and what cannot be done. In essence these differences in values shape our visions, which in turn become the foundation for creating our realities.

For example, those who operate from values of power and control and those who operate from values of learning, creativity, and harmony have different attitudes about what is possible. The "power and control people" tend to come from a place of scarcity and pessimism, whereas the learning, creativity, and harmony types come from abundance and a belief that anything is possible.

Thus, community conversations sound different when they are positioned in power and control instead of learning, creativity and harmony, as illustrated in Figure 6.

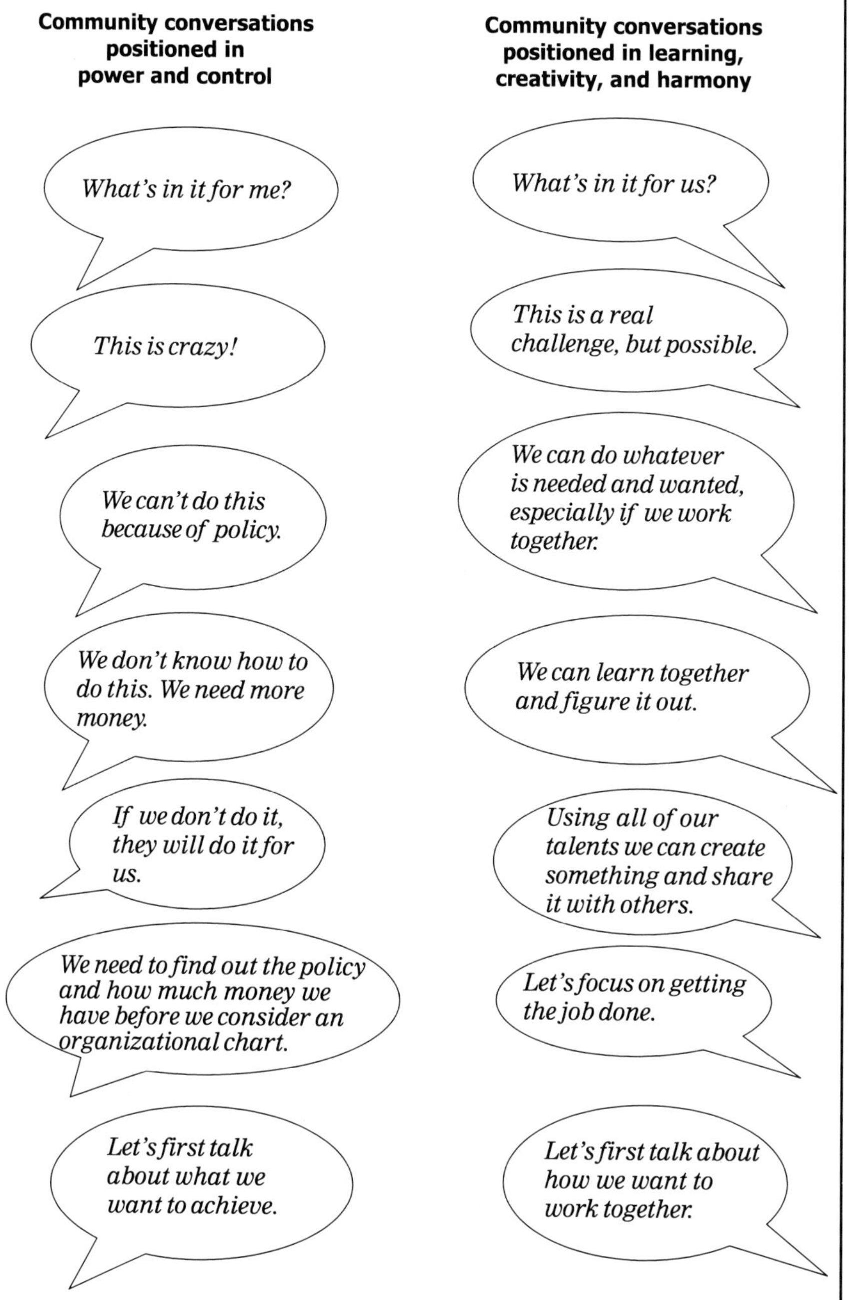

Figure 6: Community Conversations

The reality that people want is reflected in the principles mentioned at the beginning of the book. **These principles represent the fundamental beliefs about what is possible in communities**:

- Every community and community member has the capacity to be different.
- You can start anywhere and with whatever you have.
- Healthy communities and healthy individuals are interdependent.
- Respect for the dignity and worth of people promotes equal opportunities and access to resources.

These principles/beliefs reflect a set of **values** which we consider crucial for getting communities to work differently and more effectively (See Figure 7 on the following page).

Individually and collectively we reflected on what was happening in pockets of our organizations and communities that were working well. We found that when people lived values such as personalization and inclusion, cooperation and collaboration, mutual learning, empowerment in governance, and appreciating complexity and integration that the work changed and changes began to take place for individuals, organizations, and the larger community.

The idea of social capital has been around for almost half a century. Some definitions from the literature are offered below.

> The set of resources that inhere in family relations and in community social organization and that are useful for the cognitive and social development of a child or a young person. These resources differ for different persons and can constitute an important advantage for children and adolescents in the development of their human capital. (Loury, 1977 cited by Leader, 1988)

> Social capital is the capacity to create our communities through networks and the trust they engender and relies on citizen participation in creating healthy families and communities. (Coleman, 1988)

Principles and Values for a New Reality

An Overview of Social Capital

It DOES work when, instead of:	There are VALUES of:	Which creates the SOCIAL CAPITAL:
Objectification and Separation • People treating each other as objects. • People separating themselves from one another.	**Personalization and inclusion**	• Personal capacity to be in relationships. • Trusting relationships, bonds of reciprocity, and identification with community.
Competition and Protectionism People needing to win at others' expense, to feel safe.	**Cooperation and collaboration**	Enhanced community capacity and collective strength (e.g., Together we can do it; we can figure it out").
Having and Knowing People needing to have all the answers.	**Learning through doing, participation, and mutuality**	Awareness of the capacity for learning together, mutual learning, optimism, increased risk-taking, and increased participation.
Control People needing to control others through use of power.	**Empowerment in governance**	Purpose and agenda are defined and driven by the community.
Simplification and Fragmentation People wanting quick and easy solutions.	**Embracing of complexity and integration**	Culture of awareness and inquiry.

Figure 7: Values That Contribute to Social Capital

In terms of purpose, social capital has been offered as a comprehensive explanation for why some communities are able to resolve collective problems cooperatively and others are not. High levels of social capital appear to be linked to measures of community health. These include enhanced economic development and educational attainment, and lower incidence of violence and other crime, teen pregnancy, child abuse, and neglect and developmental delays.

Different authors have addressed aspects of social capital by defining single concepts and relating the importance of these concepts to the building of social capital. Usually their interest in relating a particular phenomenon to social capital is shaped by the discipline they represent. For example, human capital and social capital (Coleman,1988; sociology), economics and social capital (Knack and Keefer,1997; economics), governance and social capital (Evans, 1996; Smith,1997; economics), motivation and social capital (Brehm and Rahn, 1997; Portney and Berry, 1997; political science and psychology), learning and social capital (Wilson, 1997; urban studies), to mention a few.

Other authors have expanded on this initial thinking and relate social capital to economic development, physical development, and broader notions of community development. Operationally it appears that social capital is individuals interacting with each other and producing activities that result in products and outcomes for the common good.

Much of what the social capital literature describes fits with our "success" experiences within community. Like other proponents of community development, we came to regularly refer to and use "social capital" language. However, we came to the realization that the social capital literature does not go far enough. The presentations on social capital are, at best, vague on how and why it worked and how it could be created. The literature often left us wondering whether or not each author spoke of the same phenomenon. Despite the long-standing history of social capital, perspectives on social capital in the literature are fragmented, discipline-specific, related to the authors' particular interests, and basically lack an integrated perspective with consistent definitions and meanings of social capital language.

Beyond counting evidence of specified indicators of social capital (i.e., economic development dollars, new partnerships, and new programs), there are few explanations or little documented evidence of its functions and dynamics. On the other hand, there are good concepts and ideas worth considering when attempting to understand better ways to develop social capacity. As it turns out, these concepts provided a language for us to talk to each other about what we were experiencing, and prompted new ways of thinking about social capital and how it works. However, if we are to create healthy families and communities then we need more than our vision of healthy communities. We need to break

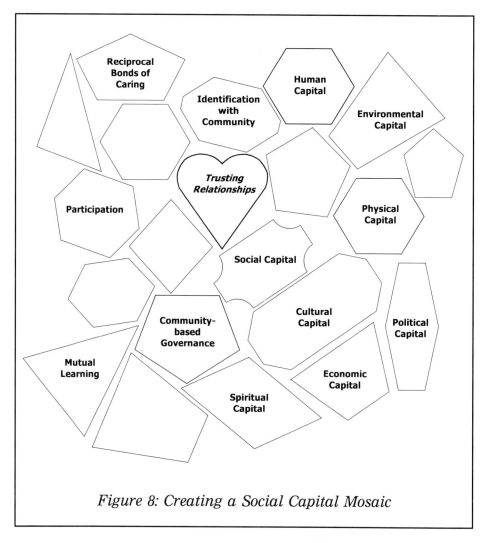

Figure 8: Creating a Social Capital Mosaic

out of our limited views of what is possible and create a different context and process for recreating communities. In our view, this was going to take a more comprehensive and complex notion of social capital (See Figure 8).

Our dialogue about social capital is what led to the identification of pieces in a Social Capital Mosaic. We created the idea of a mosaic to capture the many aspects that appear to play a critical part in creating social capacity and to offer a more complex integration of these aspects.

The pieces of the mosaic focus our attention on critical aspects of community and community development. Very simply, **the pieces of the Social Capital Mosaic offer ideas of important things to consider when creating or enhancing community capacity**. These pieces of the Social Capital Mosaic float on top of a community that is grounded in the principles and values mentioned earlier. There is no presumed relationship between particular values and individual pieces of the mosaic. They simply co-exist. The principles, values, and pieces of the mosaic resulted from our experiences of success when creating a different reality within various community settings.

By broadening our perspective of community we increase the potential for understanding the complexity of interactions among pieces of the mosaic, values, and how community enhancement works. This larger view opens up new possibilities in figuring out what might be done to address situations that are tame, wicked, messes and wicked messes in communities. We suggest that we are better able to create the kind of communities we want by using a different process while:

- being in relationships,
- identifying with community,
- experiencing reciprocal bonds of caring,
- engaging in mutual learning,
- having a community-based governance, and
- enhancing or creating different capitals.

Social capital is certainly a key community asset which can be grown in any kind of community whether it is a work, family, social, or larger community. Social capital is the extent to which a community is involved in making "things"

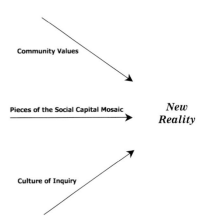

Social Capital Mosaic

Community Values

Pieces of the Social Capital Mosaic → *New Reality*

Culture of Inquiry

When It Works...

happen within relationships and through social interactions. Community members come to identify with and care about each other, and care about what they are doing together.

It is not just a few people making things happen. The building of community capacity involves many members of the community making things happen. However, it is more than the doing of events; it is doing events with the purpose of enhancing or increasing the capacity of community that in turn creates more events and more community capacity.

Personal Story

The William Whyte Community School is an example of community partnerships and social capital creation. The community school project is a partnership involving the City of Winnipeg, Winnipeg Child and Family Services, and the Winnipeg School District. The intent is to integrate service providers to meet the educational, social, and health needs of community members. The idea is to learn, work, and problem solve together to assist each in reaching his or her full potential.

The school hums day and night. The myriad activities created by the community might include:
- Coffee Club
- Council Meetings
- Homework Club
- Reading Program
- Integrated Special Education classes
- Nutrition Breaks
- Breakfast Program
- Cultural Arts and Awareness
- Alternative School for Grade 8
- Family Pow Wow
- Volleyball

The school walls are alive with pictures of individuals and groups of community members. Expressions of talent are also posted on classroom and school walls. The computer room has children surfing the Net, making charts and graphs, or working on reading and math programs.

It is within the hum of relationships that new ideas are co-created, shared, and developed. The ideas which take shape in the way of projects, activities, and meetings become the vehicle for new relationships, skills, projects, activities, and meetings. The individuals and groups evolve and function at higher levels, and they, in turn, create more relationships, learn more skills, and create bigger and better projects.

The more we get together, the more we do; the more we do, the more we get together. Social capital represents those resources that come out of our being involved and working with each other.

We assume that the complexity of social issues and of building healthy communities requires a comprehensive understanding and effective synthesis of what the community needs and wants. Therefore, we need conceptual and analytical tools that will aid us in understanding the many pieces of the Mosaic and the complex dynamics of the issues needed to address them.

One of the tools that has been available in the social capital literature is the idea of different kinds of capitals representing the assets of the community, including human capital, physical capital and economic capital. The different capitals are useful in terms of thinking about what kinds of initiatives are needed to further community development within a particular community.

We have added more types of capitals and discuss them on the following page in order to explain their influences within communities simply by their presence or absence. We suspect that even more capitals will be identified as the dialogue continues.

Economic Capital
Economic capital is represented by economic transactions that result in economic viability and profitability. Economic transactions include purchasing, selling, banking, contracting, marketing, financial management, budgeting, investing, and taxing. In essence, economic capital requires the exchange of goods and services for future payment and includes the extraction of taxes. Economic capital is most clearly evidenced in the amount of exchange of goods and services, which is closely tied to human capital. Unless community members have the intellectual and social skills required to buy, sell, budget, manage, invest, and bank, there is limited human capital capacity and ,therefore, limited economic capital and capacity.

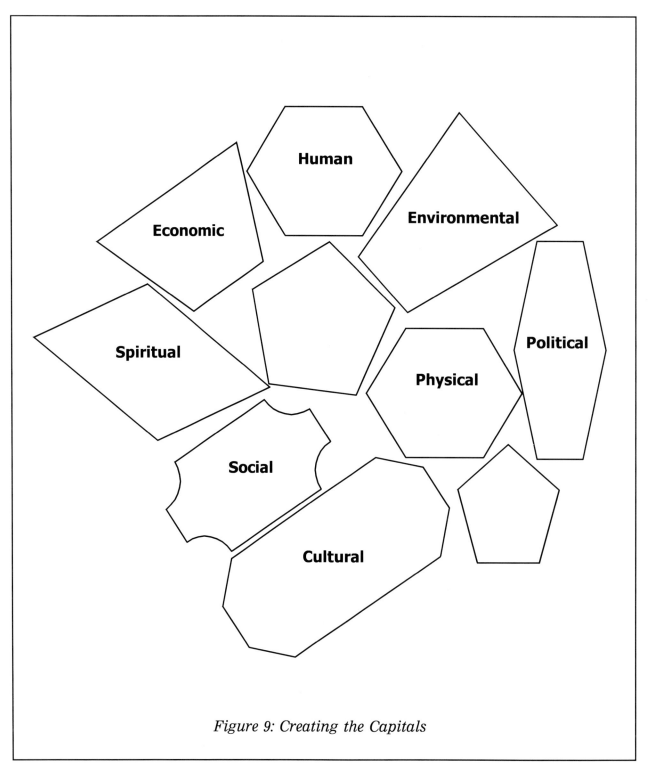

Figure 9: Creating the Capitals

Physical Capital

Physical capital refers to tools, machinery, and productive equipment. Physical capital includes all equipment that is required and utilized to facilitate production of all aspects of the community. Often taken for granted, physical capital is sorely lacking in underdeveloped communities (e.g., snow removal equipment, road building equipment, house building equipment, transportation equipment, teaching equipment, medical and dental equipment, banking and postal equipment, communication equipment, fuel pumping equipment, and so on). This equipment is so much a part of daily life in urban communities that not having such resources is unthinkable. Without physical capital, life chores take longer or simply go undone, leaving the community without access to what are now generally considered normal everyday conveniences.

The most critical aspect of having equipment is that it opens up and makes available information. Access to information is fundamental to the creation of basic health conditions. Without access to information about what is healthy and how to do things differently, progress is impeded. Physical capital represents the difference between living in the Stone Age and living in the advanced technological world. Without physical capital, it is not possible to create an advanced environment, surroundings, and way of life. Simply put, new ideas — even good ideas — cannot be implemented without the proper equipment; that equipment provides an important link to information and healthier living.

Human Capital

Human capital is manifest in the skills and capabilities of people. Human capital represents an ongoing investment in personal growth that allows people to act in new ways. A comprehensive way to think about human capital is to think of it as growth and development in the physical, social, emotional, cognitive, and spiritual aspects of life. The greater the growth in all aspects of life, the greater the personal health of individual community members. This health in individuals represents the workforce that can think, plan, implement, and work together to enhance families and communities.

In order to have human capital it is necessary to ensure the availability of healthy foods, housing, clean water, and sanitation. Further, it is necessary to have training and education that is provided through good parenting and education programs. The socialization through education prepares individuals to: appreciate and manage their emotions, read and write, think and reflect, understand themselves and others, and interact in ways that enhance relationships and promote working together. Without these human capabilities, economic deals are less likely to succeed or simply cannot be made, equipment cannot be run, and production within communities is limited.

Environmental Capital

Environmental capital is represented by the natural resources embedded within the environment and in turn represents the natural capacity of the environment to sustain life for people and other life forms. Each environment has its own natural beauty. It may include rugged terrain, lots of water, and few trees. Each environment has its repetitive weather systems which affect what can grow, how travel takes place, and what access is available to distant ports and airways. The environment dictates and limits what can be created within it without bringing in outside resources. For example, in deserts things can grow once the water problem is taken care of. Not many people venture out in February in northern parts of our provinces, and in recent years large community complexes have been built so that communities can participate in different sports for longer periods of time. Historically, areas without fish and animals were usually avoided as it was difficult to sustain life.

Political Capital

Political capital is represented through political ideology, political parties and associations, and political activities. Political awareness and skills, contacts, networks, and activities that prompt greater political awareness are political capital in the making. Political arenas are filled with small and large groups of relationships and it is within these relationships that politics are born and live.

Cultural Capital

Cultural capital is built by creating and using cultural products that serve to maintain a culture. Art, language, traditions, rituals, and symbols used by community are ways that promote identification with the community or raise the profile of the community. Loss of language through oppression or loss of communities from disease are detrimental to cultural capital.

Spiritual Capital

Spiritual capital is another community asset. Spiritual values, symbols, rituals, and traditions are used daily and generate more spiritual capital. Recently, communities have been searching for ways to build spirituality in an effort to combat what is perceived as a loss of spiritual capital.

While social capital and the other capitals are all important pieces of a Social Capital Mosaic, there are other pieces which represent or affect relationships. We found that in conventional communities and organizations relationships were of little interest and were never addressed even when they were problematic. However we place **trusting relationships** at the heart of the Social Capital Mosaic and consider them to be essential for increasing social capacity. It is within trusting relationships that the creation of events, and therefore the enhancement of capitals, occurs. Furthermore, trusting relationships are relationships where there is a **mutual caring** for and **trust** in the other. This prompts an **identification with the community** and other community members.

    Participation is also included as a piece of the mosaic because it is through participation that relationships are built. Active participation also enhances **mutual learning** and is the key to **community-based governance**, other key pieces of the mosaic.

Summary

Thus far in Part Two we have suggested that to deal with the complex messes of our time we need to create different realities in our organizations, families, and communities. To do this, different values and more than a single concept of social capital are needed to create the new reality. Therefore

Relational Factors in the Mosaic

Trusting Relationships

we propose that the Social Capital Mosaic is a collage of ideas to which attention must be paid when recreating community. The central piece of the collage is trusting relationships. Because trust is formed within caring relationships and fosters identification with community, trusting relationships is related to reciprocal bonds of caring and identification with community. Participation is another key aspect in building relationships, mutual learning, and community-based governance.

In a Different Process

Participation looks different in those communities that experience success. In 1982, Carol Gilligan created waves with her book *In A Different Voice*. Her book spoke pointedly to gender differences in values and how boys and girls thought and acted differently in terms of taking right action or being ethical. We want to borrow her metaphor of speaking in a different voice because we believe that living the Social Capital Mosaic requires speaking in a different voice. A different voice represents a different ethic, ethos, and set of values — a different place to come from. It is this different place that directs a different process for community members. Community members engage in assessment, reflection, and creation of the pieces of the Mosaic as the design of the community evolves and takes form.

Personal Story

In the First Nations communities in which I came to work, the opportunities were endless in terms of community enhancement. The question was, "where do we begin?" We decided to begin with the individuals and their personal learning about their health and well being. Education, training, and consultation sessions were all presented with the understanding that the conversation would eventually lead to individual stories and life dilemmas. It was necessary to listen, to care, to offer empathy, and to prompt other ways of living in terms of daily events and life chores. It sometimes looked like a mix of teaching, therapy, and play. At other times it looked like insurmountable hard work. Most of the time it looked impossible, but we were engaged in creating something in a different and very personal manner. We knew that we could go it together.

We propose that community members engage in a process that creates a Culture of Inquiry, a Culture which values and fosters learning and understanding for all community members. In this culture there is commitment to discovery and creativity in addressing the issues of the day, whatever they might be. In essence, the Culture of Inquiry is a collective of thinking individuals committed to learning and understanding, to discovering and creating together what is needed and wanted within the community — no small task!

Creating a Culture of Inquiry is different from creating a bureaucracy and, as noted earlier, requires a different template and set of values in order to proceed. Some initial efforts in capturing what is involved in creating a Culture of Inquiry have been referred to as "creating dialogue." However, we think it is more complex than creating dialogue and not easily captured. Here is our attempt in light of our experiences (See Figure 10).

There are a number of aspects to the Culture of Inquiry, the first being that it is a process of listening, processing, integrating, and understanding. In conducting this process, one pays attention to the content or substance of what is happening, the patterns of communication amongst community members, the tone of the communication and of what is happening, and the community's beliefs and values. This process occurs at different levels: the individuals, the groups, and the community as a whole.

The effect of being involved in this attending and community-focussed process brings an awareness to community members of their collective thinking, learning, and understanding, and of discovery and creativity. This awareness reinforces the inquiry process, prompting more awareness as the community develops.

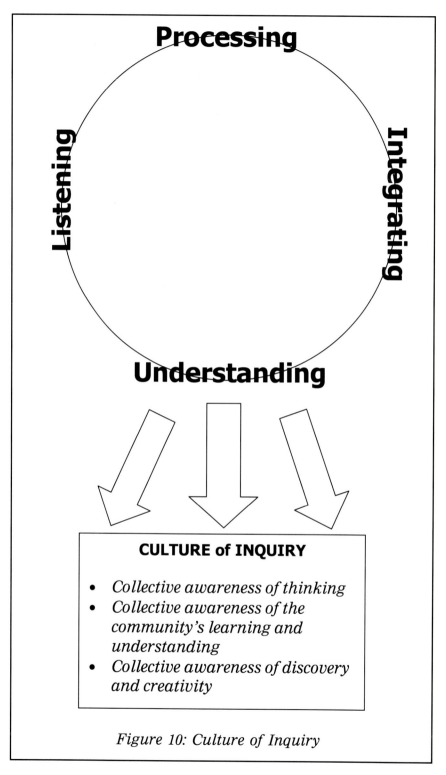

Figure 10: Culture of Inquiry

Creating a Culture of Inquiry involves many individuals and groups. One way to think about this is as a matrix of interacting systems with their members. Interconnected and interdependent relationships develop out of these systemic interactions, and the work of the community is done through the efforts of all members in the matrix. To create the collective thinking required to support these efforts, an awareness by members of all the players is one of the first things that must happen. This awareness is key to the entire process of growing the community. The larger community needs to **know many, if not all,** of the players and what each has to offer.

These ideas about the important beliefs and values, the pieces for a Social Capital Mosaic, and a process of inquiry result from our experience in working with communities that are doing it differently. These glimmers of success have shown us a different way, which we present in Part Three.

Part 3

Living a Social Capital Mosaic

In our discussions with community members about their visions of healthy community, we have found that they are also clear and consistent about their values for operating in relationships. As noted in Part Two, these values include:

- personalization and inclusion,
- cooperation and collaboration,
- mutual learning, and
- empowerment in governance.

When living these values, people feel energized, connected in a meaningful way, part of something bigger, and more hopeful and more committed to participating with others in creating what matters to them. There is an air of excitement and expectation that carries them forward to action.

We share these values for living in community and the vision for healthy community. We have had many positive "community" experiences that have whetted our appetite for communities living differently. However, many of our early experiences were "happy accidents" until we came to the understanding that communities could be more intentional and make choices about how to live in community.

The discoveries that we introduced you to in Part Two — the Values, the pieces of the Social Capital Mosaic and the Culture of Inquiry — are our findings from our process of inquiry. For us, the **values** are the foundation for living

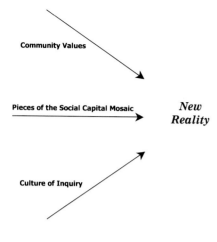

Community Values

Pieces of the Social Capital Mosaic

New Reality

Culture of Inquiry

differently and, therefore, the place where you start the inquiry. The Social Capital Mosaic is the community's manifestation or implementation of values, and this can only be intentional when there is community awareness.

We struggle at this point. How do we communicate that living these values is a creative and dynamic process that comes out of learning together in relationships? In Part Three, we discuss and provide stories about what living these values looks like in practice when the community is creating their Social Capital Mosaic. However, our discussion focusses on what needs to be created to live the pieces of the Mosaic while maintaining a place of inquiry. These stories and discussions are not meant to be prescriptive, only illustrative of what it may look like when community members are working and learning together to actualize their vision. The stories may illustrate other aspects of the Mosaic and process of inquiry. We invite you to create your own illustrations and join us in this discussion of living in a different way (See Figure 11).

Personalization and Inclusion

The value of **personalization and inclusion** shifts us from the predominant practice of objectification and separation that we discussed in Part One. Instead of treating each other as objects, staying separate from and mistrustful of each other, and focussing on deficits rather than strengths, we suggest that living differently requires that community members wade into relationships in a significant and meaningful way. This means that community members commit to building and enhancing both our existing relationships as well as being open and pro-active in creating new relationships. These relationships support us in being more inclusive and included within our families and communities.

The value of personalization and inclusion manifests itself in all pieces of the Social Capital Mosaic, but most particularly within the pieces that we have called **Trusting Relationships**, **Participation**, **Identification with Community** and **Reciprocal Bonds of Caring**. We discuss Trusting Relationships in greater detail below and the other pieces within the later discussion on *Cooperation and Collaboration*. However, before we embark on these discussions, we need to first discuss the personal capacity

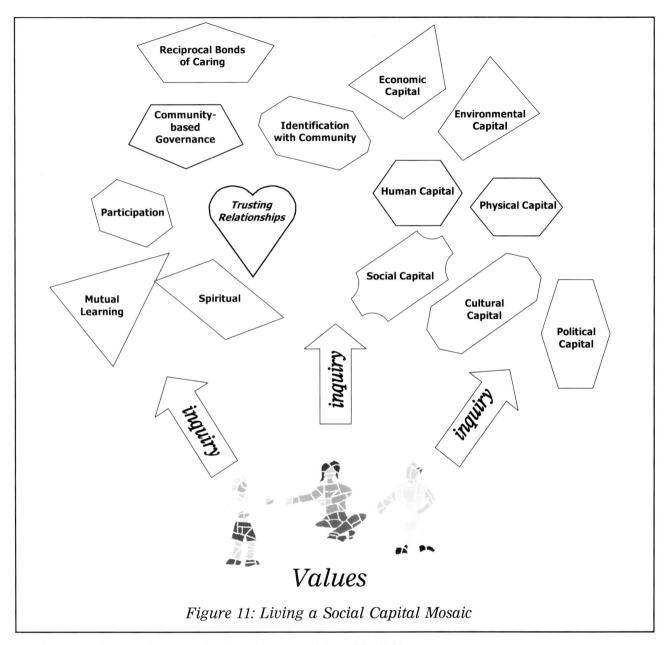

Reciprocal Bonds
of Caring

Economic
Capital

Environmental
Capital

Community-
based
Governance

Identification
with Community

Human Capital

Physical Capital

Participation

*Trusting
Relationships*

Social Capital

Mutual
Learning

Spiritual

Cultural
Capital

Political
Capital

inquiry

inquiry

inquiry

Values

Figure 11: Living a Social Capital Mosaic

to be in relationships and, thus, be capable of building a Social Capital Mosaic.

As we shall discuss in Part Four, if you wish to live differently — to be a part of living a new reality — you must start with your self. Personal capacity to live differently requires that you have the skills as well as the commitment to be in relationship with others, to engage in social, organizational, and community activities, and to conduct activities that require specific abilities. We believe every community and every community member has the capacity, or the potential to develop the capacity, to create health for themselves and for their families and communities.

Personal Capacity To Be in Relationships

To build confidence and participation in social interactions and relationships, specific individual behaviours, skills, and attitudes are required. The mastery of these skills builds the level of trust in self and others high enough to cross over the threshold between non-participation and participation. Some of the skills are basic but must be present in personal interaction repertoires before trusting relationships can be built. We have clustered the skills into four categories:

1. **Emotional Intelligence Skills**
   - awareness of self and others
   - self-confidence and control
   - capacity to have and express empathy
   - capacity to have and confidently use social skills, including acknowledgement of others and effective communication
   - ability to trust others and to be trustworthy
2. **Cognitive Skills**
   - divergent thinking, critical thinking, analytical thinking and integrative thinking
   - literacy
3. **Self and Family-Care Skills**
   - nutrition
   - hygiene
   - recreation and play
   - child care and home management skills
   - home financial management skills
4. **Work and Community Skills**
   - organization skills
   - planning and problem-solving skills
   - work-specific skills such as trade, vocational or professional skills

In essence, healthy and well-functioning individuals possess a **human and relational capacity** that enhances the capacity for social capital at the neighbourhood level. Healthy individuals have a greater likelihood of creating healthy families and communities. It is equally true that unhealthy families and communities do not create healthy individuals. The health of individuals, families, and communities makes a great deal of difference in terms of building a Social Capital Mosaic. Having said this, personal capacity cannot be achieved by "directive" nor through "one-off" services and programs. It is necessary to work with the inter-relationships amongst personal capacity, community health status, and the pieces of the Social Capital Mosaic.

In many isolated, oppressed, and disadvantaged communities, personal capacity is limited. Even in communities endowed with money, education, and social status, interpersonal capacity may be limited. A Social Capital Mosaic cannot be created where personal, and thus community capacity, is limited. Another way of stating this is that unhealthy communities create unhealthy individuals who do not have the personal capacity to be in relationship. Without community members who can be in relationship with each other, a healthier community cannot be built.

In the First Nations communities in which I came to work, there had been generations of oppression and domination over local decision-making. This took the form of centralized dictation and control over local budgets, lack of quality education, health and social services, lack of local employment opportunities, a history of multiple abuses of community members to each other, substance abuse, suicide, and other side effects of long-standing oppression. These oppressive circumstances had eroded many individuals' and families' personal capacity and stripped the community of human capital.

Personal Story

We know that personal capacity and health can be learned and created in any community. Figure 12 suggests the nature of human capital factors and how they influence each other (i.e., individual behaviours and attitudes, confidence and participation skills, and trust in self and others).

While healthy, well-functioning, and skilled individuals are a requirement for creating a Social Capital Mosaic,

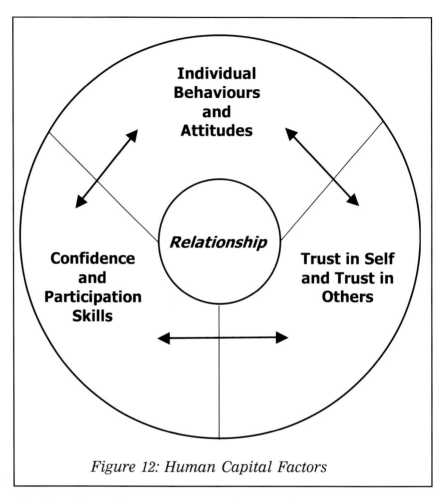

Figure 12: Human Capital Factors

having them does not ensure its creation or development. The presence of healthy and well-functioning individuals simply presents one of the necessary conditions. It could be likened to having a stack of lumber, nails, hammers, and other necessities for building a house. Simply having the necessities does not ensure that the house will be built! On the other hand, having the vision for building a house without the requisite supplies or skills will not be enough either.

Trusting Relationships — The Heart of the Social Capital Mosaic

Assuming that healthy, well-functioning, and skilled individuals with the capacity to be in relationships exist within the community, we now move on to discuss the very heart of the Social Capital Mosaic — trusting relationships. Let's look at some examples of trusting relationships:

- One neighbour tells another that her marriage is over. She and her partner need help in getting through the divorce, attending to the children during and after the process, and establishing two housing units which can meet their individual needs and the needs of the children. The neighbour responds by suggesting names of lawyers, offering to baby-sit so that the couple can work things out, and assisting in finding suitable low-cost housing.
- An older athlete, retired from competitive sports, establishes a local soccer league and coaches one of the teams. Over 200 children are involved in the league each year. Parents assist by volunteering to enrol children, organize the league games, coach teams, and make sure that all kids have transportation to their games.
- A neighbourhood group decides to take pride in their community by ensuring that the best candidates available get elected through informed choice. They organize "get to know the candidates" sessions, offer rides to those who might not otherwise turn out, and have follow-up neighbourhood discussions which focus on matching what candidates had to say with the community vision.

Trusting Relationships

In all three examples people are choosing to be involved, choosing to take responsibility for certain tasks, and choosing to engage in some activity with each other. Further, the engagement takes place within some structured relationship — friends, neighbours, or community membership. The interaction within the relationship relies on peoples' abilities to participate in activities and social exchange.

Let's be clear that, when talking about relationships, we are including all the different types of relationships we are part of in our daily lives. In fact, we are rarely out of relationship. There are relationships with family members, school personnel, church members, and even the gas station attendant. The characteristics of these relationships are different, but they are all still **relationships**. In turn the interaction, which takes place within relationships, enhances the abilities of those involved and results in some specific social actions that benefit participants. The more people invest in their social exchanges, the more is created from these social exchanges. This is the essence of creating a Social Capital Mosaic; you see it, or its absence, and are a part of it every day.

It has been argued that this ability to create social capital by commanding resources through social networks must be separate from the level or the quality of existing resources. Otherwise, social capital is just a statement about how success breeds success. To some extent, it may be a phenomena of success breeding success. However, the ability to command existing resources within communities should actually result in a new level and quality of resources. It's not what the community has — it's what they do with it! In Figure 13, the level of capitals is represented by the size of the circles. When enhancing social capital, the circles always get bigger regardless of the level at which you begin.

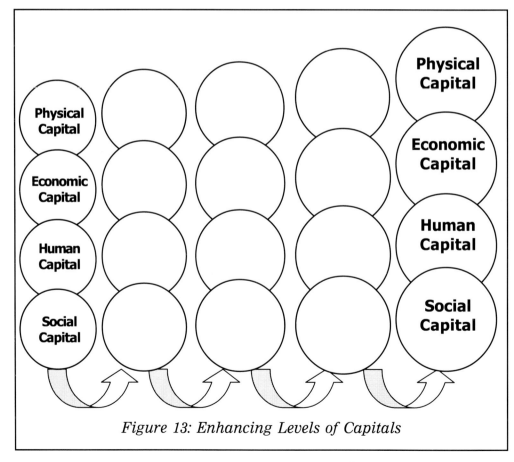

Figure 13: Enhancing Levels of Capitals

How is Trust Related to Relationships?

Trust is one of the frequently mentioned, critical aspects of social capital described in the literature. Trust has been related to creating civic cooperation and economic development. We extend this line of thinking and believe that the potential or capacity for the development of a Social Capital Mosaic is dependent upon having or creating trust with self and others.

> So many people have been deeply damaged during this lifetime. It is such a privilege to be part of their stories and lives, although I sometimes find their stories to be overwhelming in the moment. Repeated experiences of physical, sexual, and emotional abuse, the lack of adequate food, clothing, and housing, the suicides and murders that occur in a given week or month, all are taken in stride and dealt with in some humbling and fumbling way.
>
> Through their sharing and my direct participation in the community, I am a part of these humbling and fumbling experiences. Some days, when I leave for the airport to return to my world, my heart is heavy, and I can hardly let go from holding someone's hand. I know that as I leave I am trusted with their stories and lives. This trust is fragile because acting on what I know must be carefully considered. This is a very different world compared to the one in which I spend most of my time.
>
> I live with a foot in each world, stepping carefully, and hoping that I can trust myself to do the best thing given the circumstances. What I do is based on long conversations that occur within our trusting relationships. It is within these relationships that we figure out what to do. We know that sometimes we will keep silent in order to honour the trust we have for each other. We also know that, as the trust builds, the silence will be broken. When it is broken, it will be broken in a united voice.

Consider the following levels of relationship that exist within communities and work organizations: isolation, association, affiliation, collaboration, co-creation, and synergistic and interdependent (see Figure 14). The trust factor is critically and interactively linked to the nature of different levels of relationship. **Higher levels of relationship have higher levels of trust.**

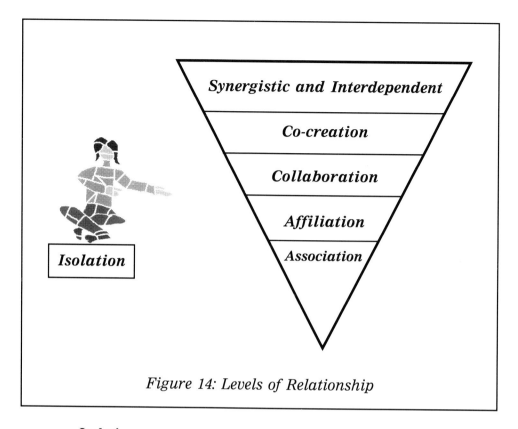

Figure 14: Levels of Relationship

Isolation

Isolation is being in a state of non-relation. Those in isolation are not interacting with others and do not have information about others. The isolated individual, family, or community operates alone — separate and without consideration of others. The isolated condition is one in which there is only a reference to self. It seems likely then that those who are in this state experience little trust of the self in relation to other and, therefore, have no trust of the other. In isolation, there are feelings of alienation, separateness, and being out of touch with what is going on in the larger environment. Because of the lack of trust, there is no reaching out to be in relationship.

Association

Association is the first level of being in relationship. Those who associate with each other have a loose connection that may or may not be collectively purposeful. When we walk to town or to the store and meet and greet each other, there is an association. When we attend meetings, we are there together and may associate with each other but may not be united in our attention and actions. In associating, there is a recognition and acknowledgement of the other, but little united purpose and sharing of goals and objectives. There is limited trust in association. There is just enough trust to speak and be in the same place together at the same time.

Affiliation

Affiliation involves a loose kind of relationship. When we attend the same party, go to the movies together, watch the Super Bowl game on television, or attend an activity as a group, we are affiliating with one another. Affiliation requires a liking, a "birds of a feather" kind of relationship, where there is enough goodwill and liking to do something together. Affiliation requires a formulated degree of trust. We don't just go anywhere with anyone. We don't just invite anyone into our homes for a party. There is the presence of liking and trust beyond what is required to simply cross each other's path.

Collaboration

Collaboration is working jointly toward some goal, objective, or outcome. We collaborate when we help people move to a new home, build a community park for young children, or conduct a fund-raising project. There are many aspects of trust that matter when collaborating: trust that "we can do this," trust that "I can do my part," and trust that "others can do their part." It is the collaborative level of trust that is required in order for the most basic of organizations, including community organizations, to function. When collaborating, there is enough trust in each other to know that what needs to be done will be done, albeit within the dictates of the job and work environment. Collaboration is required in work projects and in work environments where each has a part to play and each is necessary to get the work done. While people work together to do the work, there is limited building on each other's work.

Co-creation

Co-creating relationships are those in which members bring something new into existence. Co-creation requires working together and building with what the group brings to the situation at hand. The outcome of co-creation is something new and different which is the result of the joint efforts, abilities, and new-found capabilities of the group's members. In a co-creating process trust abounds! There is trust in the self and in others to operate at a co-creating level. There is trust in the process of creation; there is no blueprint of "what is to happen" and "what is being created" because it has not yet been created. Contributions are given, accepted, and rejected in the spirit of coming up with the best outcome. The level of trust is such that, when an idea is rejected or modified, it represents a choice that has been made in the best interest of what is being done jointly. Such choices are not taken as personal affronts.

Probably the best way to express this level of relationship is that care for each other is abundant. There is a high level of participation and strong identification with what is being done and with those doing it. The writing of this book is such an enterprise. Building on each other's ideas abounds. Changes in wording are just changes in wording. The levels of participation vary with each person relative to their circumstance, and participation is valued rather than tallied. The rules for authorship have been *created for this production* and reflect the spirit of the content of the book rather than the rules of the academy or conventional rules of publication.

Personal Story

> Eight women are hiking in the woods and staying at a cabin that belongs to one of the women. Late at night they hear a crashing on the door. Many are frightened and alarmed, shouting, "Oh dear, it is a bear and we will be eaten alive!" "Not to worry," says one of the women. "We will simply go out the back door." "There is no back door!" exclaim the women. "Where do you want it?" asks the one woman.

Synergistic and Interdependent

Synergistic and interdependent relationships are those that rely and depend on the combined efforts of all members to create what is beyond the capacity of the individual members or smaller groups of the whole. There is a level of trust such that people feel safe to check out meaning, to expand on ideas, to modify ideas, or even to take the project in a completely different direction with the blessing and understanding of the group. These people build rocket ships together and then ride in them! The parts they are not directly working upon are entrusted to the others — completely! To take the analogy home, let's look at the parenting relationship. When one partner is not at home, the "away" partner knows that the other will parent in a way that speaks for both of them. This trust and mutual support of the other enhances their parenting and promotes the health and wellbeing of the children beyond what has been discussed between them. In synergistic and interdependent relationships, everyone is flying, winning, and having a good time.

> In a small western Canadian city a group of men meet regularly to have their vision turn into a reality. Their vision is a place where men can come together and celebrate each other. They want this place to be one of celebration and also a safe haven where men can reflect and heal.
>
> This small group has secured a wilderness site on which they are building a sweat lodge, a covered cooking area, campsites, and recreation areas. Out of this relationship, the group has expanded and is currently co-creating a health conference for men to be held on a weekend in a camp setting. It is the intention of this conference to raise public awareness and understanding of men's health issues and to rally support for men as they face their health issues.
>
> The group meets on a regular basis. Work is done in small committees. The group size varies from meeting to meeting. The work continues as they face challenges of learning together and trusting that the project will be the success they want it to be. Their goal is to have 150 participants from communities in and around the city at their conference.
>
> The process is challenging as members come and go. These men are building trusting relationships while working together on the conference. This, in turn, is creating care for and identification with each other and the project. While there is a collective intelligence, there is mutual learning in action that is having the effect of building their human capital, physical capital, and economic capital.

Personal Story

For example, they have had to learn about becoming a society and how to get their society number. They have had to learn how to get donations in the form of goods in kind (e.g., free advertising from local television stations, radio stations, and local newspapers as well as dollar donations for conference costs). This has taken them into the world of governance around private societies, a world of red tape, run-around, and conflicting messages. Their commitment to each other shines.

Partnerships and Trust

While healthy people think they operate from a place of trusting most of the people most of the time, they probably are more discriminating from situation to situation. Because of this discrimination, it is necessary to ensure that the trust level required to accomplish what needs to be done is in place. The trust level to associate together is different from the trust needed for collaboration. It is different again for what is needed for co-creation, and different again for synergistic and interdependent relationships. **A "one size fits all" trust level is not discriminating enough when creating a Social Capital Mosaic.** Further, the trust and relationship level required will depend on the challenges being undertaken in the context of building the Social Capital Mosaic.

There is considerable discussion in the literature about the need for partnerships in building social capital and, within those partnerships, the need for a critical level of trust. However, there is little discussion about the fact that some partnerships can be fairly loose agreements, while others define complex relationships that require agreement on a number of factors. For example, two dance partners only need to agree on "the dance being danced." Dancing partnerships do not take a great deal of effort as the dance being danced is usually determined by the partner designated to "take the lead," all within the norms and rules of dancing. Life partnerships, on the other hand, are more complex. Life partnerships require some level of agreement on beliefs and values about the nature of partnerships. More specifically, life partnerships involve agreement on common goals, sharing the risks and profits of the relationship, and a commitment to each other within the relationship. Even more demanding in life partnerships is the need for partners to recognize that the partnership is evolving as they live it. The nature of the relationship required for dancing versus the relationship necessary for life partnerships, and their implied trust levels, are quite different.

While predictability is an important dimension of trust, **the key is to be able to trust under the condition of unpredictability.** Trusting your life partner or colleagues to come up with something that works for a situation is not about knowing the "solution" that *will be generated*. Rather, it is **knowing that your partner will come up with something that *is acceptable* to all in the absence of knowing what that is!**

The level of trust needed in communities is more like that of life partnerships. Communities require some level of agreement about community beliefs and values, common community goals, sharing of the risks and profits, and a commitment to each other and the common good. Often communities reflect certain beliefs and values. For example, a community valuing religion and education might be evidenced in the presence of church/temple activities and

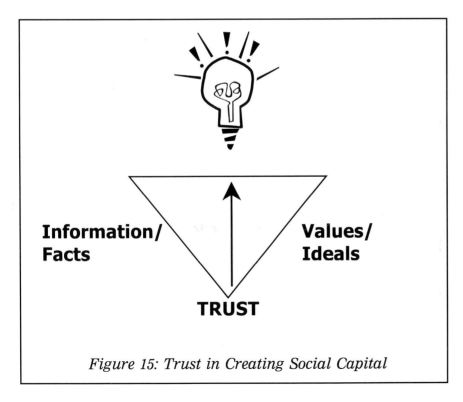

Figure 15: Trust in Creating Social Capital

education activities. The extent to which they support each other's religious and education activities would suggest common goals. The extent to which they collaborate and share resources, rather than compete for resources, would suggest a sharing of risks and profits. If a temple burns down and the community gets behind replacing it, there is clear evidence of their commitment to each other to realize their common goal of being a religious and educated community.

One way to think about trust in terms of creating social capital is to see it as the platform or foundation upon which a precarious process is balanced (see Figure 15). The apex of the triangle balances on the "U" in "TRUST," making it clear that the process rests on the collective **you** and on the individuals trusting each other!

When viewing Figure 15, one begins to understand how a lack of ideas, never mind good ideas, can occur. So many factors need to be present. Ideas spring from the

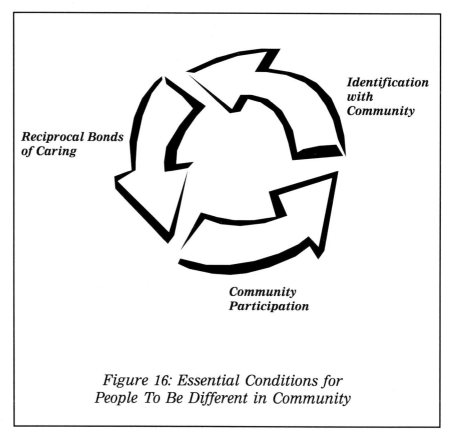

Figure 16: Essential Conditions for People To Be Different in Community

consideration of facts and information relative to existing values of the community. Creating ideas within relationships involves the incorporation of information and facts in light of the values and ideals held within the community. There is the need for **mutual trust** in order to **play with facts and information in light of shared values and ideals** which enables the generation of **ideas**. Unless ideas are co-created and implemented, there can be no social capital!

The values of cooperation and collaboration contrast with the dominant values of competition and protectionism that we discussed in Part One. Instead of turfism and hierarchical structures that create and sustain power differentials, mistrust, secrecy, and competition, we believe that the shift needs to be made to embrace equality, information sharing, and collective strength and power.

As with the other core values, the value of cooperation and collaboration is manifest in all the pieces of the Social Capital Mosaic. However, it is most critical to the pieces that we have called Participation, Identification with Community, and Reciprocal Bonds of Caring (see Figure 16). These values also lie at the core of healthy community, and enable people to move through the different levels of relationship.

One condition is not more important than another and each condition affects how the others build more identification, bonds of caring, and participation.

Cooperation and Collaboration

Personal Story

I have been involved in or witness to numerous discussions, debates, and arguments around how resources should be allocated to the many areas of public need that governments traditionally define for communities. What I noticed about these events is that, despite the fact that the people sitting around the table are skilled, knowledgeable, and talented, they are typically a homogeneous lot. I also notice that the tone of most discussions is competitive, defensive, and protective. People make arguments as to why their slice of the pie should be preserved or added to and how much more significant it is than the other slices of the pie. Even when the entire pie has been threatened, people seemed unable to drop their special interests in the interest of working collectively to save the pie for the future.

It hasn't always been so. A number of years ago, I was involved in the development of public health policy concerning the health of women. Using the techniques of a "search conference," women from many different backgrounds came together to share their views and ideas about what mattered to them in their lives. Women who were Aboriginal, single parents, refugees, immigrants, sex trade workers, health care workers, and academics worked with each other to identify both common ground as well as unique needs. Somehow, the participants came together in a spirit of mutual respect and honouring of self and other so that the strength of the collective emerged.

Identification with Community

Identification with community occurs when members have an identifiable community to which they have a sense of belonging. Identification involves feeling proud about being a member. This identification with community and other members prompts shared visions and goals. Members are willing to work together to realize the vision and reach the goals. Identification with community fosters a desire to stay in the community rather than move on. There is an attitude of "Let's do it" and "What a great place to live."

Personal Story

It is a feast day. Everyone in the village will come. They will be dressed in their finest dresses and outfits. The dinner is scheduled for 5:30 p.m. My daughter and I are working with the local committee to put on the feast. We bring in roast chicken, remove the bones, and arrange it nicely on platters. We go to the school to prepare the gym for the event. The tables are put up and places are set at the tables. It is 5:30 p.m. and we are not ready. Nobody looks alarmed. The word is sent out to the community that dinner will be at 7:00 p.m. We continue to prepare the food. Around 7:00 p.m. the food is ready. People are now standing outside the gym door. The food is placed on the tables. At 7:30 p.m. the doors are opened. Eighty people come into the gym and sit at the tables. There are couples, young people, old people, families, and single persons. Small and younger children are left to run around the hall as they wish.

Following a brief grace people begin to eat. In thirty minutes the feast is over and people begin to leave. Once people have left we clean up the gym. The tables are taken down, the leftover food is taken to those who need it, and we return to our residence followed by happy, smiling children who tell us what a nice feast it was. Indeed it was!

Reciprocal Bonds of Caring

Reciprocal bonds of caring are represented by members of the community caring about and for others in the community and knowing that they are cared for by others. Caring is evident when people share equipment, take food to shut-ins, include others in family outings or other activities of inclusion, and do things with or for others. Community caring nurtures participation! The participation offers a kind of leadership that serves others and the community. Very often such acts of leadership empower others to act, and things begin to happen.

I am in a small community with my daughter and grandson. My daughter is working with a youth theatre group and I am there to support her and to assist in the care of my almost two-year-old grandson. My daughter goes to the theatre group practice and I am caring for my grandson.

Three teenagers come by on their "quad." A quad is a four-wheeled source of transportation. The quad is motor driven and the wheels are very big and fat. Sometimes entire families get on their quad and it is not unusual to see dads driving around with their children at the end of the day. The teens ask if they can take Jared for a ride. I agree and say that they must drive slowly and carefully.

After an hour the teens have not returned. In another thirty minutes my daughter returns and wonders where Jared is. I explain the situation and we agree that she should drive around the community in the truck and see if she can locate them. She returns to our residence as she cannot find them. At this point we put out the word and just before community members are about to join in the search, the teens come over the hill on the quad. Jared is beaming from ear to ear and has orange colouring around his mouth indicating that he has been drinking orange pop. They took good care of him.

Community Participation

Participation is face-to-face membership and interaction in community-based activities. Decision-making meetings, social events, recreational activities, educational workshops, and so on, all provide participatory democratic environments which transform the way people behave in the community process. Participation in successful activities is self-reinforcing and has the effect of making individuals want to be involved again. This prompts people to step forward and bring others with them into the next round of participatory events.

The "soon to be elected" chief, his wife, and young son are on my porch. I answer the knock on the door. The chief asks, "Can we come in for a visit?" I respond by saying, "Of course. Can I fix you some tea?" Once the tea and cookies are in place, we begin to chat about the community, the theatre group's play, the youth, their concern for this newest child and the weather.

As the chief is about to leave he says, "The children love to come to this place. Be careful to not let them stay too long. Some are needed at home."

I thank him for this reminder and they leave. Two of their other children are in the theatre group's production.

Three years ago three of my neighbours decided to plan a "block party." They undertook to arrange a number of special events, many of which were geared to families, and invited the participation of neighbours within a four block area. Following the special events, a potluck barbecue was held and we were entertained by musicians drawn from our community. It was a huge success and my children eagerly anticipated it the next summer. Again, the same three people undertook the organizing and it was a success. Clearly people looked forward to the event as an opportunity to meet their neighbours in a family-friendly, child-safe, social context.

As summer started this year, my children asked "when is the block party?" and I phoned one of the key organizers to inquire. She said that, although she and the other two leaders wanted to participate, they were reluctant to take on the full responsibility for the event again. I offered to become more involved and we agreed to contact other people in the neighbourhood to invite their participation in organizing the event. Seven people have now come together to plan the party and new ideas and connections with other members of the community have been brought into the fold.

What I have noticed about this process is that many of us in the neighbourhood had assumed that the same people would take responsibility for leading the block party this year. Only when asked and encouraged to participate did people come forward, although they did so enthusiastically. I also noticed that as more people became involved, more options and connections became apparent to all of us and the load was shared. I did not know two of the new members, yet we quickly established common ground around our children, pets, and work and now greet each other warmly when we see each other. Interestingly, we have shifted our approach this year and are asking more from the members of the neighbourhood (e.g., to bring things to offer to others). I'm curious as to how people will respond.

Embedded in all three conditions are value differences that become the source of most tension and conflict. To overcome or resolve these value differences requires a condition of listening to and understanding the other. Listening and understanding are more likely to occur when people care enough about each other to listen, share a commitment to a vision and goals, and interact with each other on a regular basis.

On a small northern Canadian Cree Nation reserve people live in isolation and are rarely seen out of their houses except to attend church, buy groceries at the Northern Store, and attend a few community meetings. In an effort to get the community members involved with each other and to generate an identification with the community and participation, a Summer Games was set up by a theatre youth group. Competitions in different events — tug of war, baseball, Olympic events of a humorous nature, eating events, and a community picnic — provided opportunities for community members of all ages to come together and play. After this event, the youth put out a call for a Community Parenting Committee. The committee was needed to assist the youth in their theatre group. The response was tremendous. All parents who had attended the Summer Games came to the meeting and donated their talents toward fundraising, costumes, and chaperoning. This Parent Committee continues to be a source of support for the parents as well as the theatre group.

What happened here? A shift in the level of relationship? Identification with community and sense of belonging and meaning? A new experience of being together?

Personal Story

Opportunities to meet, to play, and to get to know each other lead to other opportunities, which create awareness on the part of community members of other members, their likes and dislikes, their beliefs and values, and their perceptions of what is needed and wanted. As a result of this awareness, community members are more likely to get involved and participate with each other to address their needs and wants. In our experience, this is true of all kinds of communities!

It works the other way as well. Lacking a sense of belonging and caring not only increases a lack of involvement and participation, it increases our need to get and take whatever we can get by competing. For example, in a large organization where there are isolated workers (i.e., those who stand apart from the group, those who do not speak out, those who do not attend the organizations's social events), it is less likely that workers will be meaningfully involved in the work of the organization. They do not relate to each other and are not involved with each other. As a result, they do not share ideas about what is possible. Often such an organization is fragmented and has a number of players who will compete with each other for whatever gains can be made, such as promotions.

When the three conditions of identification with community, reciprocal bonds of caring, and participation are present, community members can more effectively deal with the healthy tensions and conflicts that come with the need for collective learning and value-based decision-making to create community change.

Community Capacity for Change

A fundamental belief of those who work and live within the new reality is that **the community and community members have the capacity to change**. The attendant value to this belief is that it is important to have and use this community capacity. Living this perspective involves envisioning individual and community strengths and capacity for growth. All personal and communal assets are viewed as having the potential for enhancing the everyday lives of community members, thereby ensuring the growth of the community. Other fundamental beliefs of this perspective include respect for the dignity and worth of people, honouring their right for self-determination regarding their life choices, and promoting their entitlement for equal opportunities and access to resources.

The actualization of these beliefs and values in practice

promotes peoples' strengths and potential and expands the community's capacity to care for its members. The focus must be on utilizing community members' capabilities and ensuring that they determine the values that will be the foundation for their community.

Once community members are clear about the values they want to live, they can begin to figure out what their choices would look like when actualized in the community. To do so, they must see and understand the alternative way before they can live it. Living the alternative way is simply the practice that fosters the empowerment of individuals, families, and communities. Rather than having practitioners or professionals do the work to or on the community, the community members work together to put into practice the alternative ways based on their collective values.

From Community-focussed to Community-driven
While some practice models are more respectful of community and collaborative relationships than others, we believe they all fall short in promoting community involvement and asserting complete autonomy for communities in addressing their own needs. **Such approaches to practice still separate the service users and residents from the service providers.** While most would insist that there is no blueprint or specific framework for the community practice, the mutual processes that practitioners engage in, the relationships they establish with community members, and the way in which they go about planning rarely promotes solutions designed to fit the circumstances of the community's unique situation. In other words, no amount of community-focussed practice rhetoric, such as teamwork, volunteer outreach, or exchange of ideas, encompasses a redefinition and expansion of the practitioner's role to that which is needed. **What is needed in communities is for practitioners to become living, practising members of the community.**

To be a member of the community does more than redefine the professional's focus. It redefines the nature and quality of membership for all community members, particularly for professionals, thus creating a new reality for practice. In this reality, community change is accomplished through full and equal participation of

Community-focussed	Community-driven
Prevention and promotion	Collective responsibility for community
Partnerships with professionals as the leaders	Community leadership
High degree of participation	Involvement of wide range of community members and community ownership
Ongoing relationships	Mutual relationships based on respect and trust
Professional, group, and community support opportunity to participate	Community determines the roles and relationships of professionals to the community
	Community determines resources to best meet needs
Focus on strengthening family and community capacity to care for members	Focus on support and fostering community leadership and shared responsibility for strengthening and sustaining community health and wellbeing
Work within community	Join community in its endeavours

Figure 17: Community-focussed vs. Community-driven

community members. Through this full and equal participation, the community drives change. The changes within the community in turn create or enhance the Social Capital Mosaic.

Some of the differences between a community-focussed orientation and a community-driven orientation are presented in Figure 17. The community-focussed orientation perpetuates a reliance on support from professional service systems and practitioners. Such support fosters control and dependency rather than empowerment of individuals and families to generate their own solutions to their community issues. As a result, community members are seen as clients and consumers of services rather than as citizens with talents and capacities to contribute to the community's development.

The community-driven approach, on the other hand, is one that resists a reliance on professional service systems and professionals for support. A community-driven approach requires human service professionals to promote community leadership and governance over community resources. The practitioner's role is no different than any other community member in that their competencies are viewed as resources which the community may draw upon. All community members are practitioners and must continually examine their motives and actions to ensure they are congruent with the aims of the community. By ensuring this equitable and wide representation of community members, the potential for sustained commitment and ownership of community issues and solutions becomes possible. Ownership for the wellbeing of the community is located within and among community members. The community-driven approach holds the potential to foster community leadership, citizen ownership, and locally-determined responsibility and accountability for the health and wellbeing of community members.

Need for Community Process
In order to address community change, it is important to recognize and emphasize healthy community processes. As noted earlier, the process requires being involved in relationships while learning together and creating what is needed and wanted within the community (see Figure 18).

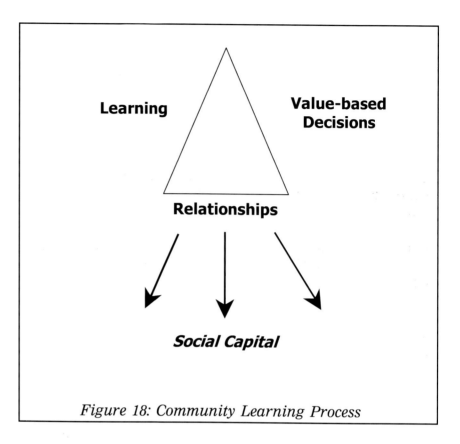

Figure 18: Community Learning Process

Learning partnerships that focus on recreating or enhancing health in the community must first foster the participation of community members. This community learning participation is necessary for making value-based decisions about ideas generated by the group. In essence, the generation of ideas and the determination of which ideas will be enacted determines what, when, how, and by whom something will be done.

Mutual Learning

The value of mutual learning contrasts with the predominant value of having and knowing discussed in Part One. This value shift takes us from a place of people needing to have all the answers, or hiding the fact that they don't have the answers, to the awareness of the strengths and opportunities available in learning together.

Shifting to a Learning Orientation
As noted earlier, collaborative, co-creative, and synergistic relationships are the context for collective and mutual

learning. In order to foster mutual learning (as opposed to having and knowing), we must understand that:

- we cannot become what we need to be by remaining the way that we are, and
- the **learning** concepts are fundamentally different than the **having and knowing** concepts.

For example, collective and mutual learning has a different orientation to learning than having and knowing. In mutual learning, learning is a continuous process within daily life. It is co-creative because it happens in the presence of and with the support of others. Learning is broad, encompassing skills, knowledge, and attitudes. It also involves a continuous circle of knowledge, practice, action, and reflection, also known as "think, do, learn." This contrasts with having and knowing, which emphasizes formal training events as tools to ensure people adequately implement new procedures or learn specific skills or techniques.

These different orientations to learning directly affect decision-making processes. In a learning orientation, decisions are created within the relationships of community participants. The processes and subsequent decisions are value-based, collaborative, reflective of the ideas generated by the group, and in alignment with the goals and vision of the group. Decision-making processes create an opportunity for people to learn together and are distinguished by high levels of trust; individuals may make decisions in support of and with the support of the group.

This contrasts with the having and knowing orientation in which the "top dog" calls the shots and may or may not incorporate the advice of others. Decisions are often defined by policy, procedures, and positions in the hierarchy. Decision-making processes are oriented towards "facts" and "logic" as defined by the decision-makers, and are often competitive and biased towards action (and biased against reflection). Furthermore, when things go wrong, controls are increased.

People speak and practice differently when they are operating from these different orientations. There is either pessimism or optimism, rule-boundedness or creativity,

Figure 19: Speaking and Practicing Differently

disengagement or engagement, competition or collaboration, and control or empowerment. Notice the differences in Figure 19 above.

Within a learning orientation, people practice very differently. They create a shared vision, engage others, and emphasize strengths. They embrace diverse participant perspectives (including the outliers, eccentrics and risk-takers) towards achieving the shared vision. In contrast, the having and knowing orientation results in people being focused on following the rules. People become self-protective and disengage from each other and the work. The experts and prophets are presumed to be the only ones who know the answers.

When a learning orientation is put into practice, it becomes apparent that there are no experts, only learners. People position themselves as learners and are excited by their potential and the potential of others. Diverse perspectives are honoured, and expansive and creative thinking is encouraged. Thoughtful crafting of new strategies is based on reflection and rethinking. There is no one right way. The way that is chosen may be different within and across communities.

Accountability is actualized through community evaluation research and community action. Community research is viewed as getting information to inform the community about what needs to be done. When research is evaluative, it informs the community about what works and what doesn't. The community can then take responsibility for what works and what doesn't; this puts them in a position to learn from what happened rather than to lay blame.

In contrast, the having and knowing orientation embraces its experts or "those who know." They are distinguished by their position or status in the hierarchy and often by their formal credentials. As long as there are experts, those who are not experts tend to "park themselves" at the door of their work. What they need to do is captured in the rules of policy and program so there is no need to bring *themselves* to work. New actions are actually new reactions. Accountability is defined by policy. Evaluation reports are generated externally by experts, and "wrong-making" justifies what happened and "clarifies" who is at fault.

In the example about the good playground that was no longer available or suitable for your family, imagine what it would be like if you came from a place of learning rather than knowing. You would seek out an alternative space for spending play time. You would create options for yourself and your family. Now let's take this a step further. Instead of waiting for a precipitating event to prompt your inquiry into alternative places to play with your children, what would it be like to be continuously open to learning about other places to play. You would be open to hearing other suggestions. You may pick up some information from the local parks department. You may ask people for their ideas.

You may organize adventures with your kids to check out other play places in your community. In this example, knowing served a purpose but learning was the route to creating alternatives.

Using our parenting program example, imagine what it would be like if you came from a "continuous learning orientation." With a continuous learning orientation, your program is likely going to be different every time that you offer it. You may not even offer a "program" at times as you seek to address the needs of the people in your community in a different way. You work with the participants to identify their dominant needs and go from there, working to enhance capacities beyond skills. Every day is a new day and presents you with new opportunities for your own and others' growth.

Learning Community

Because learning occurs within contexts that involve relationships, we need to recognize that optimal organizational or community learning is more likely to occur in groups or teams. People who collaborate can learn from each other; this builds human capital and synergy, both of which drive social capital.

This has altered our perspective on the locus of learning; learning is a process that takes place in a participation framework, not in an individual mind. Learning is mediated by the diversity of perspectives among the co-participants. While it is possible that one or several of the co-participants may be the ones most significantly transformed by their participation in the learning process, it is the community learning context and process that is the crucial locus and precondition for such transformation. As such, it is the community that learns. Communities that learn together are transformative.

Learning in community, or mutual learning, implies at least two things:

- **Learning is best facilitated in the presence of, or with the support of, others.** At the centre of the learning community are the relationships that exist between its members. Relationships between people create an energy that does not exist within an individual. The relationships allow for and stimulate inquiry, challenge, new levels of understanding, and use of new ideas to bring about better outcomes. Being prompted to reflect and think assists us in questioning and learning about what we don't know. This can only be done in the presence and safety of others.

- **For systemic and lasting change to take place, the learning opportunity must be mutual, inclusive, and self-reinforcing to the community members and the community itself.** There is a potential for conflict between two groups if one group is doing "the learning" and another interrelated group is not participating in the learning. For example, those in the place of learning may try to engage those in the place of having and knowing and both may experience frustration with the activity or inactivity of the other. Those who are in the place of having and knowing, given that they are more prone to feeling fear and confusion, may experience feeling "small" and inadequate as they sense the risk of the exposure of their "not knowing." A continuous learning model, operationalized within committed communities is a "great equalizer." It is also the best route to vitality and viability. By ourselves, we are limited, but together we can be something wonderful. This "wonderful" outcome is experienced by individual community members, and there is a group pride which surpasses any individual's experience of success. This sense of accomplishment is reinforcing, and new learning initiatives are welcome.

I remember a university colleague commenting on a student's work by saying, "There is a germ of a good idea here somewhere." I always remembered this statement and considered it a mean-spirited and vicious put-down. However, at the time I didn't understand why I thought that. What I have learned by working in communities is that just about everything begins as a germ of a good idea and that, if left to be developed and acted on by the one person who thought it, not much would happen in any community — or university.

When working in community, the good idea does not belong

Personal Story

to anyone; it is just a germ of an idea that has been thrown out into the universe. Once it is out there, it begins to take on a life of its own as various members of the community work with it, develop it, and eventually bring their version of it into reality. The germ of an idea goes through a metamorphosis from germ to vision, vision to strategic plan, strategic plan to action/implementation, and, once a reality, it is evaluated. The germ of an idea becomes a visionary experience through the use of the group's collective intelligence. As my husband is fond of saying after we have co-created a workshop, "two half wits make a whole wit." In the case of community, many hands make light work and many heads are better than one! An example follows:

The executive director of the Awasis Agency in Northern Manitoba called to say that he had three communities that were having great difficulty in working as teams in their communities. Because of this difficulty the work of child and family services was not being done in these communities. Would we put on a workshop for them?

An easy response would have been to conduct some workshop on team building or some other kind of training thing. Instead we planned three days which involved the team members of these communities in assessing their needs and deciding as teams where they would go from here. Day One was be spent on the questions:

- Why are you here?
- What brings you here?
- What do you need to know or what do you need from each other to create safety in working together?

Days Two and Three were organized around the following questions:

- What do you want for yourself?
- What do you want for your team?
- What do you want for your community?

The premise of our approach was that their collective intelligence would likely have better insight and understanding about their issues than we would. This was coupled with the belief that they have the capacity to solve their own problems. And they did!

Empowerment Through Governance

The value of empowerment through community governance contrasts with the predominant practice of control discussed in Part One. Instead of bureaucratic hierarchies, power differentials, limited community access and involvement in decision-making, program and service-driven systems, attachment to the status quo and rule boundedness, we propose that a better way can be found through community-based governance.

Empowerment permeates the pieces of the Social Capital Mosaic that we have called **Identification with Community, Participation,** and **Community-Based Governance**. It supports mutual learning in action and the creation of collective intelligence. Below we expand upon the piece of the Mosaic called Community-Based Governance and speak to alternative perspectives.

Public Choice Perspective on Governance

Governments are a means for individuals to act together "through institutional arrangements assigning special prerogative, or authority, for some individuals to act on behalf of other" (Ostrom, 1987). "Good" government creates the context, processes, and structures that allow for collective deliberation to determine which alternative will achieve the greatest public good. Governments committed to good governance create the open space for meaningful governance structures and processes to emerge at the neighbourhood, community, municipal and regional levels. In our view, this is also smart government. It recognizes that social problems are complex and beyond the capacity of provincial or federal governments to solve.

Effective solutions to wicked messes like environmental degradation cannot be owned, prescribed, or dictated by governments. Citizens themselves must take responsibility for recycling materials and disposing household chemicals properly. The problems of community development in the inner city, of school and social welfare reform, of violence and addiction, and many other problems are simply too complex for our traditional government structures to address. Regulatory and therapeutic solutions cannot treat people merely as passive victims, needy clients, or righteous claimants. Such approaches do not work as policy or prove effective as politics, when community members are disillusioned with the capacities of government and the techniques of experts. The need for new approaches in governance is long overdue, and we must learn how to mobilize local wisdom, community assets, and civic capacity.

Bureaucracy Model	Public Choice Model
Individual interests and needs must be set aside in the interest of the masses.	Individual interests, needs, preferences and lifestyles are important to understand; without this understanding it is not possible to understand groups, communities or societies.
Those elected to power have the duty and authority to speak and make decisions on behalf of all individuals.	Individuals have the capacity and should be given the opportunity to speak on behalf of their interests; communities have the capacity to self-govern.
Individuals are fundamentally self-interested and cannot be expected to act in the interests of the group.	Individuals are essentially rational; given adequate information and opportunity they are able to work together to make decisions for the greatest public good.
Mistakes must be avoided; these are best avoided through control.	The fallibility of individuals and their collectives provides the opportunity for them to learn and change in light of their experiences.
The availability and delivery of public goods and services must be standardized and uniform; uniformity is more efficient.	Due to the diversty of individuals and their collectives, there are diverse requirements for public goods and services; in accommodating this diversity there is more effective use of resources.
Multiple and overlapping layers of governance structures are inefficient and costly; larger amalgamated and consolidated structures are efficient.	Multiple and overlapping layers of governance structures are more efficient and effective; they create the opportunity for individuals and collectives to have a voice and select the most appropriate public goods and services for their communities.
Rules allow for predictability, consistency, and control; people need rules as they want to be told what to do and how to do it.	Rules are to serve the processes of governance and are continuously subject to change.

Table 1: Bureaucracy Model vs. Public Choice Model

A model for governance congruent with our experience of creating social capital is the Public Choice model. Underlying this model are fundamental beliefs about:

- the significance of the individual and their interests,
- the capacity of the individual to act in ways that support collective interests,
- the capacity of collectives to self-govern, learn, and change, and
- the rules that exist only to support collective decision-making and action and thus are subject to change.

The differences between the dominant hierarchical, bureaucratic model of governance that we discussed in Part One and the Public Choice model are outlined in Table 1.

The Public Choice model is a learning-oriented model. People have the capacity to act rationally. They have the capacity to consider and rank alternatives by learning more about the alternatives and reordering them as may be required. Information is essential to the exercise of rational thought, and people learn from their experiences of trying out new and different solutions. While people are considered rational, it does not mean they are infallible. However, fallibility provides the opportunity to analyze, deliberate, reconsider, and alter in light of new information and learning. The public choice perspective is one of life being a "provisional experiment subject to change in light of experience" (Ostrom, 1987).

Public choice advocates argue that "rules" for governance and decision-making can and must be formulated for various governance structures and associations. More importantly, they argue that when rules no longer work to bring about the greatest good, they need to be changed. The social contract needs to be examined, the incentives and sanctions need to be altered, and the monitoring must be more accountable. Such changes will involve conflict, but public choice theory views conflict as a learning opportunity that has the potential for creating better alternatives and solutions.

In essence, those who share these public choice values believe that communities have the capacity to govern and change themselves. Community involvement is fostered because communities know better what they need and want. It is important for community members to exercise their prerogative through voting, purchasing, accessing solutions, or seeking redress against those who violate individual rights. The diverse interests and preferences of individuals bring about collective decisions to create the greatest public good.

Multiple and overlapping levels of government bring the most appropriate provision of public goods and services to communities. The current-day practice of amalgamations and consolidations is creating structures that further the distance between policy makers and definition of needs, and ever larger and more removed governance structures. Multiplicity, diversity, and overlap are better because they create more access to and for individuals and more opportunity to engage at the meaningful and personal neighbourhood and community levels. The irony is that, contrary to what the advocates of the bureaucratic model say about the inefficiencies of many smaller, diverse, and overlapping governance structures, the research demonstrates that these structures are more efficient and certainly more effective in addressing the needs of the community and in reacting and responding to both threats and opportunities.

We cannot realistically expect that the dominant governance structures are going to fall or be modified significantly in the near future. The current system of governance is unable to respond to community needs due to the lack of identification as being on the same team as their clients, lack of functional communication, and absence of trust among the public and private agencies that are involved. How can you trust and work with people you never, or hardly ever, see? How do you get government personnel to understand your community needs when they live 500 miles away? How can relationships be personal when contracts are defined as being between agencies and government rather than between people of government and people of agencies? This raises the question of **whether a community within restrictive governance structures can protect themselves while creating a Social Capital Mosaic.** We have come to believe that different models of governance can co-exist.

I worked on a project in the northern part of my province. The project was defined and directed by the southern urban headquarters. As I met with staff to gather their views and opinions on a number of matters, the most common refrains were that the South couldn't possibly understand what the real work in the North was like and that the Southerners couldn't and wouldn't be able to do the tough work of the North. In many pockets of the North, the workers in this organization felt powerless and ineffective in their work. The formal structures were plagued by low staff morale, high staff turnover, long term vacancies, and loss of confidence. It seemed that these structures were largely overburdened and ineffective. Despite this, however, I was struck by the resourcefulness of the people within some communities. People who had expressed frustration with their work lit up as they spoke about the groups or teams that they were a part of within their neighbourhoods and communities. They spoke of how people looked out for each other, of how they banded together when faced with the threats of spring floods and summer forest fires, and of how they held a community folkfest to celebrate their multicultural backgrounds.

Personal Story

Protected Community Within Governance

We have experienced prescribed governance structures which allowed for innovative and creative things to happen. All are organizations which provided a public service and were driven by community members, including:

- a large agency reporting to a ministry,
- a small transition team within a large ministry,
- a community-based transition house,
- a specialist training unit within a large agency,
- a community centre,
- a community school, and
- a tenant association.

We think there are key aspects of these communities that contribute to the ongoing success of their operations. All the organizations shared beliefs and values similar to those reflected in this book. They operated as a community, respecting the diversity of all individuals and relationships.

They were up-front about not knowing what to do and were committed to learning together to create something more workable. The learning and the subsequent decisions were value-driven and in keeping with humanitarian principles and conduct. They realized that a key aspect of functioning differently was based on having trust for self and others. They worked daily on building and maintaining trusting relationships. Working together toward shared goals was more important than getting new positions and larger salaries. Tremendous commitment to interpersonal process and to each other ensured greater safety in finding a new way. They were collectively on a different track. They had no doubt about what was possible, even though they didn't always know what they were doing. They were committed to something better, and they would create it together.

Personal Story

Many years ago, a community I know was at a crossroads. It had a colourful and proud history, but it had become an economically depressed community. The houses and yards, once beautiful, now reflected a lack of caring and pride. Crime and violence were an everyday phenomena.

The city councillors were approached by developers who wanted to build highrises along the waterfront. "Why not?" they thought. "The community doesn't care! Besides, it might even be good for the community to have the old buildings torn down and new highrises put up."

How wrong they were! Community members found the strength to mobilize. Leaders emerged. The fight was on, and the community's voice was united and strong.

What emerged was local governance. The community took control. They fought the developers and paternalistic city council and won. They then used their new-found strength and passion to address other threats to their community: crime and violence, ill health, and economic depression.

When I became involved in the community many years later, it was a vibrant place to live. People of many colours and backgrounds lived together and created together. We initiated a drive to purchase and renovate a building that would house our community-governed health centre, family place, and many other programs that had become part of the community fabric. The community members responded with money, but, perhaps more importantly, with their time and expertise. Electricians and painters volunteered their time. Artists created works of art. Citizens donated everything from furnishings to books and children's toys. When we opened that community place, joy and pride showed on the faces of the many who had contributed.

As I look back on those days, I realize that this was community governance in action. We made many mistakes, and we had many false starts and struggles, but we did create something better together. I didn't have the language to describe it or consciousness about it then, but I am learning.

Community-based governance is just that! The community comes up with the vision, comes up with the strategic plans, executes their plans and involves themselves in some kind of evaluation of what has been accomplished.

How can something so simple be so hard? Probably it is hard because we have glorified governance. By glorifying governance we have glorified aspects of governance: being in charge, having positions, being paid more for being in certain positions, and so on. By definition, governance is simply an act and manner of governing. So far so good! We get into trouble when enacting governance. Historically to "govern," or to enact governance, means to rule, reign, or function as managers.

While local communities will need to relate to the larger government structure, as indeed it is unlikely we will do away with current government practices, only local autonomy and authority can give rise to creative solutions to local needs. Rather than impose any particular structure for governance on local communities, these "fundamental ideas" from public choice theory are proposed. They can be used by local communities to create a structure and process that works within their particular community. Such a bold move requires us to think in terms of empowerment rather than efficiency and control.

Another interesting aspect of communities who dare to do it differently is they have a champion. This leader is committed to the vision and able to protect the smaller community from the interference of a larger governance structure. The leader acts as a buffer to others within the group and deals with information that has the potential to distract the group from focussing on its vision and objectives. The leader is very optimistic and not overwhelmed by the bigness of what he or she is doing. There is no doubt that what is being tackled will be successful and that everyone involved will have a good experience. Most importantly, the leader empowers others to do what needs to be done and keeps out of the way.

> On a northern reserve the community put on a community conference. A community member, who had the idea for the conference, enrolled others in his vision. As a result, there were 12 people who came together on a regular basis to plan the event. In turn, they took leadership roles and attended to the different aspects of putting on the conference. The 12 people also created the curriculum for the conference and each person presented. Because the leadership for this event emerged from the community, attendance on the part of community members exceeded expectations.
>
> This conference led to other initiatives involving other community members.

Thinking and inquiry skills need to surface in community, and we need to suspend our old assumptions and ways of thinking. In essence, we propose that we must:

- embrace complexity,
- suspend preconceived ideas about how things are and should be, and
- develop new skills and approaches.

Having set the context for living a Social Capital Mosaic, we will now discuss how to get started. Part Four offers the new skills and approaches needed to trigger your thinking on how to live your Social Capital Mosaic, by creating and being part of a community in new and creative ways.

In Part Four we discuss ways of getting started. We shift from talking about living the pieces of the Mosaic to talking about initiating them within community. Unfortunately, we cannot give you a step-by-step program to implement a Social Capital Mosaic in your community. We have worked within many communities, and in each community a different mosaic design was created and continues to be created. In creating and living these designs, the process has not been lockstep or linear. The creating and living of a community mosaic involves an ongoing and neverending process of assessment–reflection–creation, assessment–reflection–creation, with changes along the way as needed.

The process of assessment, reflection, and creation is not a tidy process of assessment, design, and implementation. Remember that each gathering, each group of people, each individual is part of the Mosaic, and each requires connection and reconnection, involvement and re-involvement, and reminders about the vision. Therefore, the assessment, reflection, and creation necessitates a great deal of listening and processing for understanding.

This approach is a completely different orientation and approach from that often used in communities. It is one that respects the vision, yet demands the flexibility to allow anything to happen and to change course as required. The focus of assessment, reflection, and creation is on listening and watching for how things are and what there is for the

The Process of Assessment, Reflection and Creation

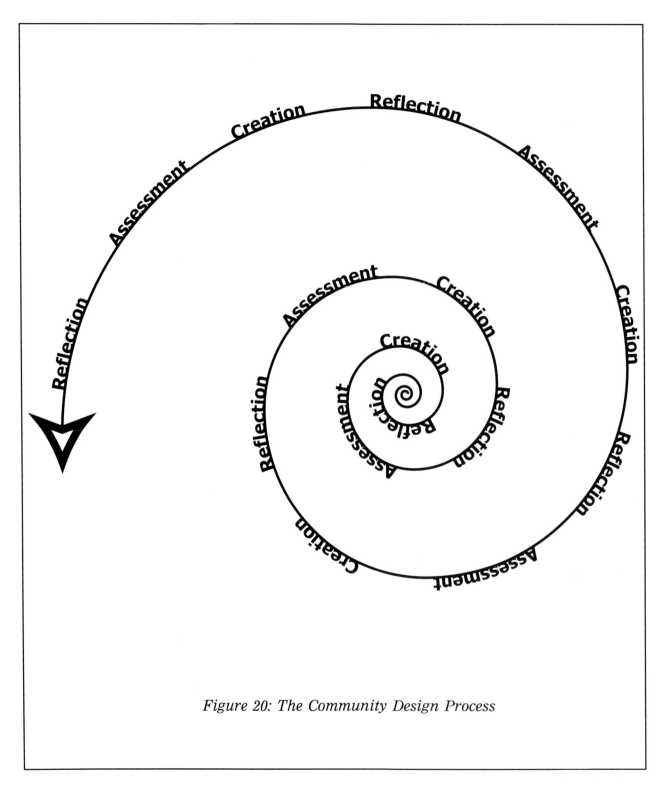

Figure 20: The Community Design Process

group or community to work with to create something different.

Know What Is Working and Is Not Working: It Starts With Me

A community's reality can only change when the community is willing to tell the truth about their current reality and recognize what they don't know and don't have. An inquiry of wanting to know and learn and an openness to anything that might come along are required. Good work rules for this process are "know that you don't know" and "tell the truth."

Community members must first identify what is and is not working for them, and how they contribute to the situation. In other words, what do community members do or not do that maintains the way things are? While this is not a comfortable process, it is crucial as it paves the way for one of our central beliefs about community and community change — **it starts with me.**

After three visits, it became apparent to me that this was a different world than mine. The long silences, what did they mean? The hard, sombre looking faces, what did they mean? Everyone coming late to all sessions and from all breaks, what did that mean? How was I going to find out? How could I ask without looking and sounding foolish or, worse yet, looking stupid? Good grief, this person wants to go home in the middle of the program. What does that mean?

Of course, the first visits were difficult because of what I said to myself. "You were wrong. You failed. You do not know what you are doing." Quit or continue? That was the question. Not being a quitter by nature, I stayed on and learned to ask "what does it mean when....?" It was a great learning! The learning was that the questions were appreciated. Questions fostered an exchange which changed attitudes and behaviour. Greater participation and trust was the result.

Recognizing the reality and how each member contributes to this reality is early evidence of community commitment. Being able to take individual responsibility points to the collective potential for taking responsibility for the larger community. Finger pointing, "ain't it awful," and other negative collective thinking are barriers to seeing opportunity within ourselves and within the community. **Don't go there!**

An agency that had a history of being oppressed, co-opted, and disempowered was plagued with employees' negative attitudes such as "we can't," "it is not possible," "he/she is wrong," and "it is not my fault." One of the first steps taken by the new executive director of this agency was to establish a rule of Be Positive. Every opportunity the director had — and there were many — he would cut off the negative comments and ask questions to promote more positive thinking and to open up opportunities. Usually he would simply ignore the negative and pose questions. "What would be a better way?" "What can we learn from this?" "Is there a way to take this forward?" "Coming at it for the children, what do you suggest?"

Telling the truth to yourself and to others can be less painful when truth-telling is framed as describing "how things are." This can take the sting out of any description because details about who is bad, wrong, and awful are not included. Through descriptive "truth-telling" we often come to know that we don't know and, better still, that we do not need to know. This is a freeing experience; it opens the door for the personal and mutual learning that is the backbone of inquiry.

One day we had a discussion about trusting relationships. The point of the discussion was not to arrive at some agreement on the definition of trusting relationships, but rather to take note of different needs with regards to trusting relationships. Only then could each member commit to respecting other peoples' needs and do his or her best to meet the needs when working together. For example, some members mention, as they often do, that they need confidentiality to be maintained at all times. If some members cannot commit themselves to maintain confidentiality under certain conditions, by mentioning their conditions to the rest of the group they can be honoured.

On another day in another community where there is a history of abuse and neglect, we had a discussion about safety and how to create safety within the group. Many women did not trust men because of their abuse by men. These women needed to get the group to respect their personal physical and psychological boundaries by making specific requests, i.e., "please do not touch me physically." Because issues of safety and trust were addressed, participation that was low, hesitant, and reluctant changed to being high and enthusiastic. This participation resulted in greater identification with the community group and mutual caring. Also, it was empowering as they figured out together that they could and would respect the other.

Questions to Ask Yourself and Members of Your Community
1. What do we like about our community?
2. What would we like to be different about our community?
3. What works and does not work in our community to create what we want?
4. What do we do, as individuals, that helps the community be the way we want?
5. What do we do, as individuals, that gets in the way of the community being the way we want?
6. How could we be different in how we work together?
7. How could we be different in how we play together?
8. What do we need to know about the others to enhance their participation?
9. How do I let others know how I like to be acknowledged?
10. How can acknowledge others in ways that work for them?
11. What skills do each of us bring to this community?
12. How can we learn these skills from each other?
13. What commitment do each of us bring to our community?
14. How can we assist each other in our learning?
15. What learning needs do we have that are immediate and how could we begin our learning process?

Understand and Live Your Basic Beliefs and Values
Basic beliefs and values are the foundation for community living. Sometimes birds of a feather flock together, and things go smoothly. However, the larger the community, the more likely it is that there will be differences in beliefs and values. While conflicting beliefs and values can be troublesome, they are a huge opportunity for learning and expanding

individual, group, and community capacity. **Essential for the community is the belief that every community and every member of the community is different and has the capacity to be different**.

When community members believe that only some people can be different, or only certain sections can be different, or only those from certain religions can be different, or only those with certain levels of education can be different, the community is limiting its capacity to change. We become what we believe and value and, therefore, must be mindful of what those beliefs and values are.

Other fundamental beliefs that promote creating a new reality include beliefs such as:

- There has to be a better way.
- We have what it takes.
- It's worth it.
- I can be part of this and make a real contribution.
- This really matters to me and my family.
- We can do this together.
- We are all part of this community and we are all equal.
- We can learn what we don't know.

Personal Story

In this community, there are different ethnic groups. The larger region has five smaller towns that are some distance from each other. Currently there are infrequent meetings with town representatives. The government funding for services is distributed by at least five different ministries within the province and also involves direct funding from the federal government.

The problems are similar across the five locations: poverty and unemployment, school dropouts, drugs and alcohol, health problems (diabetes, obesity, heart conditions, cancer, etc.), suicides, murder, lack of affordable housing, and lack of educated personnel to fill the positions in health, education, welfare, justice, and commerce.

Existing ministries designate large amounts of money to the separate locations with limited understanding of their needs and capacity. Allocations are often made on the basis of population and the "northern allowance" formulas. Occasional visits are made by "officials" who check on how the money is being spent. Community representatives meeting with the officials frequently are people who have moved from the south to the north. They usually stay two or three years, although some stay and call it home.

The current governance systems are ill-prepared to assist these communities. Community stories are not in major newspapers unless the stories involve a major catastrophe. Time-limited interventions are put in place at the time of the catastrophe and, when the crisis is over, the interventions end.

Let's just agree that this is impossible and go ahead and do it anyway. We must acknowledge we don't know how it's going to work and that it looks and feels VERY, VERY BIG!

We know we can do this together so...

Let's talk about our vision...

Let's talk about what each of us brings to this initiative...

Let's talk about our commitment to getting the job done and what will keep us off track...

Let's talk about what each of us needs to stay on-board...

Let's talk about our commitment to keeping our word.

Questions to Ask Yourself and Members of Your Community

1. What do we believe about our community and community members?
2. What some of the primary values and how do in what we do and what we do not
3. ? have the capacity? What is
4. tners within the community are
5. Are compatible with those mentioned in *All Now*?
6. Am I, and we, willing to commit ourselves to getting the job done, no matter what?
7. Who do we need to have on-side for this endeavour?
8. Do we have any lone wolves and, if so, how can we get them on-board?
9. Do we need to, and can we create, more encompassing beliefs and values that will enhance our level of participation?
10. Do we have any destructive beliefs that will or could get in our way?

Start Anywhere and Work with What You Have

Slow Down...There Is Lots of Time....You Are Changing a Culture!

Our current social problems are too complex to be addressed through quick fixes proposed by any single person, discipline, organization, or government. Our problems are complex because of interwoven relationships, and the interdependencies of systems and the people in them.

In community work it is tempting to rush in, usually alone, where angels fear to tread. There is a tendency to reduce complex matters to single solutions and to hit them over the head with the hammer we use best. Even when we do this over and over without results, we try again and hope for success.

Focus on the Swamp — the Community

It is also common to approach community issues by going to the point of conflict — the point of "noise and confusion." As workers, the conflict, noise, and confusion in communities usually get our attention. To do things differently, it would first be necessary to avoid distraction and instead examine the conditions and circumstances that are represented by the conflict, noise, and confusion. Too often we deal with the alligators when we need to examine more closely the fast-growing swamp in which the alligators proliferate. It is the swamp that maintains the conditions for the alligators that, in turn, perpetuate the community's distraction.

Get rid of the prefab community assessments. Instead, take in what is happening. Become aware of your strengths and assets. Seek to become aware of the potential capacity for human, physical, economic, political, environmental, spiritual, and social capital. Pay attention to the conversations that are happening (or not happening) and work to engage in new conversations. Do this as members and working partners in the community.

In a first meeting, the place looked like a circus, and everyone looked like a clown. The challenge was to get past the disguises and find out who these people were and what they cared about. Adults have trouble doing this so we began with the song "The more we get together, together, together; the more we get together the happier we'll be!"

After singing we looked more together and a lot happier. The mood in the room had changed, and we began to talk. By the end of our second day we cried together... and were happier still.

Individual Capacity

While working the cycle of assessment, reflection, and creation, take the time to build up what you need to proceed. Individual capacity-building may be needed for the whole group or may need to be tailored to smaller groups within the community. A certain level of health and wellbeing is needed on the part of the majority. If health and wellbeing do not exist, take the time to create them because human capacity in a community becomes the resource for further steps.

There was so much pain in the room it was the obvious place to begin.

Yet all my years in training convinced me that objectivity was important and that you must not deal with people's therapeutic needs unless you are in a therapeutic environment and have an explicit agreement of a therapeutic relationship.

I learned that this turns out to be hazardous thinking in communities. The truth is I cannot ignore the pain and act like I know nothing about what is happening. The truth is that I could be of service to these individuals and groups. By using my skills, I could assist others by increasing their personal health and their personal skills. Why am I here if I am not willing to use my knowledge and do what I can?

Key Skills for Getting Started

We think that the key skills for getting started are those required to build the Culture of Inquiry.

First is the skill of listening. This is no ordinary kind of listening, where one simply hears the birds singing and people talking. Rather, it is listening with an awareness that involves all community members knowing where they listen from and where the other members listen from as well.

The skill of listening

Knowing where you listen from means being aware of your own beliefs and values and how these beliefs and values filter your listening. When you filter, you hear what you want to hear and don't hear what you don't want to hear. Because of the matrix of individuals, groups, and communities, this becomes a fairly complex process. To have a collective awareness of listening involves increasing the awareness and understanding of how each individual, how all groups, and how the larger community listens, or doesn't listen.

Personal Story

> Everyone is talking and no one is listening. "O.K., everyone, listen up. Let's create a space in the middle of the room for 'true listening.' Each one come forward with a piece of the space that will create 'true listening.' Who will begin?"
>
> "I begin with the space of non-judgment."
>
> "I begin with the space of genuine inclusion."
>
> "I begin with the space of commitment to hearing...." and so on.
>
> "O.K., everyone, let's go to the space of 'true listening' that we have created and stretch it out to cover all of us. One, two, three, pull. Good, now let's begin our discussion."

The skill of processing information

Second is the skill of processing information. Again, the need is not only to "process" but to have an awareness of processing. Some members process more slowly, more deeply, more abstractly, more concretely, and so on. The value in these differences is only apparent when there is an awareness of these differences. Awareness of differences opens up new possibilities and new combinations for processing because community members benefit by learning from each other.

Personal Story

> Initially, I was contacted by a member of the Legislature who wanted to discuss the Awasis project in Northern Manitoba. We talked on the phone and agreed to meet for lunch. In this initial meeting, we discussed the book and considered the possibility of a similar project in British Columbia. After lunch, we parted.
>
> Several months later, I met with the same member of the Legislature and a community member from his riding in the Legislative dining room. We met to discuss the possibility of a community initiative to transform services within their region. They had read our book, *Breaking The Rules: Transforming Governance*

in Social Services, and it had been placed in the middle of the table. I wondered and asked, "How can I be of assistance?" They wanted to know what we had learned from the Awasis project. I replied that what we learned was captured in the book and that what might be created by their community would be completely different. I told them that my big learning from the project was that it was a matter of learning together and creating from that learning. I also mentioned that the Awasis project was in its ninth year; there were no quick fixes and the work continues.

The next hour was spent on getting to know each other. The conversation was rambling and personal. People expressed their struggles, their frustrations, their hopes and their visions. Our visions were similar.

We then considered "next steps" in order to move this initiative forward. The Legislative member and community member were meeting with the minister in the afternoon, and I was invited to come along. Being unable to stay I said, "Keep me advised and let me know how I can be of assistance." We parted.

Several months later, I received a phone call from an assistant to the assistant of the minister, wondering if this was the number of an author of the book and, if so, would I come to a meeting with the minister. I said, "Yes, I'll be there." The meeting was scheduled for two weeks later.

In this meeting we created the opportunity for a collective community assessment to determine whether there will be a local community, university, and provincial government partnership.

Third is the skill of integrating. Integration is the skill of putting together new and different data sets to create new knowledge. It can also involve putting new data sets together in new ways with what is already known. The emphasis in integration is on "putting together" data sets with awareness of the context. Once again, while integrating is important, it is more important to be aware of the integration and how it creates knowledge that is different from what the community knew before.

The skill of integrating

Finally, there is the skill of understanding, or the formulation of meaning that provides a collective understanding within the whole community. Having a collective understanding is a required component for living within a culture of awareness and inquiry. Foremost, there is the understanding that inquiry is required for

The skill of understanding

understanding and that understanding is the foundation for further inquiry. What maintains this collective learning process is "awareness." In other words, inquiry prompts awareness, and awareness leads to understanding.

The Andrews Street Family Centre was developed following an intensive period of community consultation. Over a period of two years, it brought together a number of existing community programs into one facility, combining them with new programs that together contributed to the development of a continuum of family supports serving all age groups. In 1994, a community survey and needs assessment was carried out. It focussed on identifying not only the unmet needs in the area, but also the neighbourhood resources and strengths that could be utilized. The Centre, incorporated in February 1995, was initially sponsored by a partnership with representation from inner city schools and local resource groups, including William Whyte Community School, the Community Education Development Association (CEDA), Pritchard Place, the Nyinakawa School, the North End Women's Centre, the Native Women's Transition Centre, the Native Alcohol Foundation, and the local Child and Family Services office. In the summer of 1995, further discussion took place to broaden the range of family support services offered. This resulted in the expansion of the Centre through amalgamation with Pritchard Place Drop-In Centre and the Moms Helping Moms project.

Using These Skills

In a culture of awareness and inquiry, all community members — the individuals, the groups, and the larger community — need to use these four skills when considering different aspects of what needs to be explored, known, or understood. Community members must attend to the content or the substance of their community: what is happening and what is not happening, what resources are available and what are not available, the nature of the issues and the evidence for the issues, and so on.

Next, it is important to pay attention to the patterns of communication that occur within and across the individuals, groups, and community participants with regards to the content and substance of their community issues. Communication patterns will vary depending on the players and the nature of the content. The challenge is to become aware of whether the substance and content matters, and if so, how. For example, in some communities, everyone knows that there is abuse of all kinds, everyone knows who participates in the abuse, and everyone knows that everyone knows. Everyone knows the pain, the long-standing effects of the abuse, and the costs to those involved. Still there is silence and an unwillingness to address the issue. What is less likely to be known is what keeps these patterns of communication in place and what maintains the silence. Are there fears of retribution? Is there a payoff in maintaining the status quo? Is there a history of abuse that distorts the community's understanding of what is normal and healthy? Is there a lack of resources for doing anything which has created an apathy in the community?

Personal Story

In one of the towns there is little interaction, few social events, and a kind of caring that occurs around disaster. When it was reported that a woman wandered into the bush and hanged herself on a tree, I wondered, "What's going on here?" When I attended the funeral and heard her life story, I realized that her life was not any easy one.

She was 22 years old. She had three children aged three years, one year, and one month. The one-year-old child had multiple handicaps and a life expectancy of less than a year. Before the birth of the third child, she spent 13 hours a day taking care of the one-year-old child because the medical system in a southern hospital encouraged the family to work together to see the child through his probable death. It was anticipated that the third child had the same condition as the second child. The woman's partner was depressed and about to leave her. The community did not have the relational capacity to support this woman, her husband, and her children. Resource people were sent in from a central agency to teach her how to care for her handicapped children but could not give relief on a sustained basis.

It was understandable that life was unbearable and that suicide had become a viable option.

In addition to the patterns of communication, there is the tone or affect of what is happening. It is important to consider and understand the tone or affect across individuals, groups, and the larger community. How individual community members feel, how groups feel, and how the larger community feels may vary. The variance may be a function of the content, or about the pattern of communication or about different community beliefs and values based on gender, race, ethnicity, and other differences. These differences matter and need to be understood.

The collective listening, processing, integrating, and understanding of the content, patterns of communication, tone or affect, and beliefs and values is the process that can lead to community awareness. The awareness of collective thinking, and collective learning and understanding offers the opportunity for a collective awareness of discovery and creativity. In essence, the awareness opens up new opportunities, different opportunities, *out of this world* opportunities to discover and create.

Personal Story

> We get large sums of money from different ministries and from the federal government. We use the money to run separate offices with separate workers and most of us see the same clients on different days of the week. What a mess! This is crazy!
>
> Let's pool our resources and set up one office. Let's rethink the work and how it can be done. Let's retrain people to work differently with the spirit of helping each other and the community. Let's coordinate our efforts and form partnerships across our ministries and with community governance. Let's fight together for the right to keep the savings that would come from this coordination and use the money for new and creative initiatives that promote health and wellbeing. Let's focus on getting things done in a new way. Let's stop focussing on who is in charge and who gets to be the boss. Let's focus on serving our community. Let's have this be a wonderful place to live.
>
> O.K.

Remember, every community and everyone in the community has the capacity. Bring them along and remember that you are creating a culture. This takes time.

Questions To Ask Yourself and Members of Your Community
1. What strengths and weaknesses do we have?
2. What local training or education could be used to enhance our human capacity?
3. What outside training or education could be used to enhance our human capacity?

4. What do I need to learn about and become more skilled at?
5. Where should we start?
6. Can we be doing other things while we increase our knowledge and skills?
7. How can we make learning in the community fun?
8. How can we make learning so much a part of what we do that no one feels stupid?
9. How can we remind ourselves that everyone has the capacity?
10. Could we set up a mentoring program where people in the community could help others learn?

Respect for the Self and Others

Respecting self and others seems like an obvious requirement of working together in community and, therefore, one that we need not address. However, there are some subtleties to respect. Because of people's different beliefs and values about themselves and others, having respect for self and others may require an overarching value: ***Respect for Differences***. Furthermore, community members cannot respect what they do not know or understand. This means that people may need to learn about differences and come to understand the differences as belief and value conflicts before they can respect the differences.

Within the discovery of differences, people find room for new opportunities. Adding to what we know or putting our knowing together in new ways actually alters what we know and how we think about things. It is within these alterations in our minds that new possibilities live!

Respect for the self and others is subtle in another way. With respect for the other comes an expectation for treating each other with basic civility and kindness. Many times we hear people not listening, not seeking clarification of ideas, and pushing their ideas over those proposed by others. Not listening to the ideas of others reflects a lack of honour or respect for others and their ideas. The tragedy is twofold: the actual treatment of each other on a daily basis and the loss of potentially good ideas. By putting ideas together, bigger ideas are born!

Personal Story

The boss in a very large agency fired people as a last resort. It was his view that through kindness people could be brought along. By respecting their ideas, the ideas could be used and built upon. This was his belief which became his reality. Indeed people did grow, their ideas were used by others, and they used others' ideas.

He was wise enough to realize too that one should be careful before firing people. Who would replace them?

Questions to Ask Yourself and Members of Your Community
1. How do individuals in your community like to be shown respect?
2. Consider general examples of times when you have had opportunities to change your mind about others. What changed your mind?
3. How do you honour others?
4. Discuss and define showing respect for differences.

Leadership

There were a number of times in the writing of this book that we wanted to talk about "leadership." Leadership, we believe, is an essential requirement for the creation of a Social Capital Mosaic. We are discussing leadership at the point in the book where we talk about getting started, because getting started in creating a Social Capital Mosaic requires a different perspective on leadership from that usually held.

There has been a great deal of comparison in contemporary organizational literature between management and leadership. Management (and, by association managers) have been framed as "bad" while leadership (and leaders) have been framed as "good." Managers live by the rules; they are hired to control and seek compliance from others in the name of the corporate or organizational agenda. Leaders, on the other hand, are charismatic and stimulating visionaries that seek to empower followers through various means such as open communication, visions, and strategic plans.

Bob is a senior manager and vice president. He prides himself on letting those under him do what they want and plays a Socratic role in supervision. In fact Bob is scared of those who report to him and is afraid that they will give him poor evaluations and possibly not elect him next term.

Mabel is also a senior manager and vice president. She prides herself on being involved in many things and knowing what is happening across the organization. She does not supervise anyone as she is at most of the meetings and can ensure that things go the way she wants them to go. She is exhausted as she puts in 60-70 hours per week. People accuse her of micro-managing and rumour has it that she will not be selected for another term because she dis-empowers people by over managing.

George is in an advisory role within his organization. This is in addition to his regular job. As an advisor he has access to the total organization. He has established small committees to attend to certain needs and disbands them when the work is done. Committee chairs are people who are closer to the issue and he attends some meetings to offer his support. He sees his role as getting resources for these special projects and to acknowledge the good work that people are doing. His personal goal is to transform the working environment of the organization so that people will work better together and like coming to work.

We have experienced both managers and leaders many times over, and in the social capital context we don't recommend that either direction is the way to go. Managers are survivors. They have a mission: to make sure that things get done in the way in which they, or others (Pals), have prescribed. They are extremely well suited to the hierarchical bureaucracies that are the dominant governance structures. People who enter into the bureaucratic governance structures with visions of offering and inspiring leadership often adapt or accommodate to the management genre in the interests of their own survival.

Leaders, at least in the contemporary sense, are more like directors or conductors. They have in mind what they want to see happen (as compared to the manager who is following the rules and orders about what should happen) and are not as rule-bound, at least on the surface. There is more latitude and recognition that people have something to offer to achieve the vision.

Despite its simplistic attraction, we found that the management/leadership model did not take us very far in our understanding about leadership as required in the creation of a Social Capital Mosaic. As we had done so many times before, we shared stories and images about "leadership in action" and tried to identify key qualities and characteristics. One of us carried the image of Moses, who parted the waters but didn't get busy managing people through the sea. Yet, surprisingly, people managed to get through the sea. Another shared the memory of a favourite "leader" who, although vested with significant powers and authority by virtue of organizational position, chose to give power to those with whom he worked. He trusted and supported them to think, contribute, create, and make a difference in the organization. Another sees leadership as a variable that floats around the organization and manifests itself at points in time through different people. Usually such leadership activities are low profile yet make a great deal of difference to the organization and the people in them. Such leadership is quiet, unobtrusive and yet "mind blowing" in terms of outcome both to the organization and to the individuals in them. Images came to mind of:

- leaders that are champions for a collective vision;
- leaders that support people in growing wings and taking flight; and
- leaders who hold back the demanding and critical hordes of senior managers to protect their people and give them the space to do their best work beyond a crisis-response mentality.

This kind of leadership is more akin to the notions of "servant leadership," as described by Robert Greenleaf and his followers or "stewardship" as described by Peter Block.

In our experience, leadership is about creating wonderful opportunities for change within organizations and for the people who work in them. No one person owns leadership, and leadership is not necessarily tied to a position or office. Leadership is manifest when people share their ideas of what to do and together build on those ideas. It happens when someone sees an opportunity to create something that is needed and wanted, and takes action to get the job done.

Twenty students enrolled in a course on ethics. They came for the answers. They came to learn about codes of ethics and standards of practice. They came to get the "right answers" about what to do.

The instructor knew that these people held important positions within their community and that they came to this course because of their need to be better at their work and to make things better for themselves and others. Thinking in "right" and "wrong" boxes was part of the issue because life is not that simple anymore. Practice issues are complex and "right" and "wrong" thinking only perpetuates ill feelings for someone.

The course focussed on becoming aware of their personal beliefs and values and where these originated. More importantly, the course focussed on having each person realize that they closed down and quit on certain issues. The ones they closed down on were those they saw as needing "right answers." By the end of the course participants realized that being ethical is a personal affair and that there are many beliefs and values which create many options and that from the options one can make a best choice.

At the end of the course almost everyone said, "This course changed my life." They went home and operated differently, providing leadership in situations that before stopped them. They received one and a half units of academic credit for the course and their communities received a whole lot more.

Personal Story

People who create or step into leadership opportunities tend to be people who:

- are optimistic and not overwhelmed by the bigness of the challenge;
- are creative and create conditions that others can step into and create;
- work **through** people to bring light and life to the collective vision and purpose (e.g., escape to freedom);
- work hard to create the context or environment for people to achieve the vision and purpose (e.g. part the waters);
- are buffers who intervene to prevent negative or limiting external conditions from impeding people's progress (e.g., keep the water from falling on the people); and

- encourage, support, honour, and respect the efforts made by the people even when people do things that the "leader" hadn't imagined, expected, and sometimes may not like.

What these social capital enhancing/capacity building leaders don't do is busy themselves with telling people what they must do and how they must do it.

These images of leadership started us on the path of thinking differently about leadership. We realized that we needed to go further than these initial images. These images suggest that a few people, perhaps vested with authority by virtue of organizational or political status, can influence and empower others in such a way as to build a Social Capital Mosaic. While this is true, leadership within a Social Capital Mosaic is all of the above and more. The "more" finds expression in stories about people who, having never spoken in a group before, find their voice and engage others to work on a community project together; of people encouraging others to get involved and trusting that the collective can find a way that is better than any one person alone can find; of appointed leaders letting go of notions of control, domination, and compliance and handing over power and choice even when the people go in a direction with which the leader is not comfortable; and of people in positions of authority not accepting responsibility for defining purpose and meaning for others even when asked to do so.

Personal Story

She worked on contract. She had the difficult job of creating changes within a large, bureaucratic system that had one way of doing things. She began by creating a team that clarified its mandate and then created a vision for living it. They became a strong and creative unit. The focus of their work was to conduct their work in a way that would work for the organization and for the people working in it. The work was not easy, the days were long, and yet, at the end of each day, the group was strong and pleased with what they were doing. It was a sad day when they were disbanded. One wonders why they dismantle units that work rather than those that do not!

How does such leadership develop? It has been our experience that leadership, which is conducive to the creation of social capital, is more likely to grow out of groups, organizations, and communities in which people:

- Share beliefs and values similar to those suggested in this book, particularly the four mentioned at the beginning:
  - *Every community and community member has the capacity to be different;*
  - *You can start anywhere and with whatever you have;*
  - *Healthy communities and healthy individuals are interdependent;*
  - *Respect for the dignity and worth of people promotes equal opportunities and access to resources.*
- Allow for their learning and decision-making to be value-driven.
- Trust themselves and each other, and work at building and maintaining trusting relationships.
- Accept that they all have responsibility for their collective wellbeing.
- Believe that leadership is shared and that the "right" leaders will emerge from the group as and when required.
- Operate as a community and respect the diversity of all individuals and relationships.
- Are up front about not knowing what to do and are committed to learning together to create something more workable.
- Believe that working together toward shared goals is more important than obtaining power over others, getting higher positions, or making more money.
- Understand that they are collectively on a different track and that they may not always know where they are going or what to do next.
- Attend to whatever needs to be done, be it small or large, and tackle it with the same attention to detail, recognizing its importance to realizing the larger vision.

People that operate in this way create groups, organizations, and communities that are safe places for risk-taking and creation. As a result people are more likely to step out of whatever prescribed roles they have had in the past and step forward to assume leadership in whatever way works for them and their community.

Personal Story

A troubled graduate student came to see her mentor. She had just taken a noteworthy job in a local community as a community developer. The mentor had attended the local community meeting and was impressed with what they were creating in this fast growing community.

The student asked the mentor what to do with a person in the community who always had to be in the centre of things, who was always talking, and who seemed to want to be in charge. The student mentioned that she thought her job was to be in charge and make things happen. "I am the designated director and that is my job!" she told the mentor.

The mentor asked her a number of questions: What is it that this woman feels so passionately about? Where might she use someone with so much energy and commitment to the community? What are her fears about this woman? What kind of response does this woman get from others in the community? Who does she work well with and what can she teach? What might be lost if she were to leave the group? How might her leaving affect others?

The discussion went in many directions and after a couple of hours the student left. As she went out the door she said, "Thank you for reminding me that my job is to get everyone on board and not leave anyone out." The mentor said, "Have fun and keep up the good work!"

The shift from having our leaders "be in charge" and "in control" to everyone being in charge and likely no one being in control, is formidable. The Kettering Foundation (1995) studied collaborative communities and reported that members of successful collaborative communities say, "**Yes, we can make a difference.**" This shift in attitude on the part of community members is empowering and enhances the capacity of the community to deal with issues. Knowing that you can make a difference bolsters self-confidence and optimism. Self-confidence and optimism raise the bar on individual performance, resulting in more effective strategies, the feeling that "we are all in this together," and the achievement of initiatives not possible by traditional methods.

The collaborative premise is: ***When appropriate people are brought together in constructive ways with good information, they will create visions and strategies for addressing the concerns of the community***. There are a number of points inherent in this premise. One is that it is necessary to bring people together in a way that ensures different perspectives and interests. Different understanding of the issues adds to the capacity of appreciating the complexity of community issues. Further, by ensuring good information, the possibility for greater insight and understanding increases the diversity of solutions. Finally, and most importantly, really good ideas grow within relationships. Therefore, the more, the merrier! Only then can you say, All Together Now…

This is not hard. Start anywhere and use what you have. We know that communities have the skills to build large and cumbersome matrixes in bureaucracies. So, it is not a matter of having skills! It is rather a matter of redirecting our skills and capacity by coming from a different place and speaking in a different voice. It is a matter of living shared values within the community and living a different vision based on those values. The values can be played out through basic and civil practices. It's simply a matter of ABC (D and E!):

- *A*ppreciate that, while the world we live in is complex, we have the capacity to create social capital and make the world a better place to live.
- *B*e personal and include others; it's a better way to relate.
- *C*ooperate and collaborate with others; it's a better way to work and play.
- *D*evelop together through learning; it's exciting and transforming.
- *E*mpower each other within governance; it's possible.

Creating Social Capital is Not Hard. It's Slow!

Don't make it hard. Play with it and create new pathways within your communities. Inside the culture of awareness and inquiry that you create, you can do anything! We know you have the capacity to do it because other community initiatives continue to thrive in Canada. You can read their stories in the Appendix.

What's Your Story?

Well, the book is done, but the dialogue just begins.

We invite you to join us by coming into our Culture of Awareness and Inquiry. Share your ideas, strategies, and stories from your experiences of enhancing community capacity and creating social capital. You can join us at **www.socialcapitalmosaic.com**. Your ideas, strategies and stories will further the dialogue on building Social Capital. They may well be used in a book that captures "What Works?: Strategies for Building Social Capital."

Gilbert Park Tenant Association

The Gilbert Park Tenant Association is a unique community development initiative. The association is in partnership with the Winnipeg Housing Authority. The objective is straightforward: Tenant Management of their housing complex. To oversee the management there is an elected Executive Board as well as an administrative staff. Community membership helps to ensure that the community members' needs are met.

The community needs are dictated by the following community demographics:

- 90% of household heads are women
- 85% are First Nations
- the average level of education is grade 8
- 90% are on social assistance

While the association looks after the physical concerns of Gilbert Park) i.e., grass cutting, snow clearing, and apartment repair), it also has a partnership with Ma Mawi Wi Chi Itata Centre, Inc. This child and family centre is located in downtown Winnipeg but locates programs within communities such as Gilbert Park. Through this partnership, local programs are created and offered. They include a literacy program and parenting programs.

The Association has a Parent Council and Youth Justice Program. They use a family conferencing model which involves community meetings, home visits, a working group to oversee the plan, and use of volunteers. The intent of the family conferencing model is to get someone in the family to be responsible and to look after the situation. Again there is an attitude that the community and families have the capacity to learn and to look after their issues.

The community association builds on the strengths of the members. Their request is, "Tell us what you have to share and we will broker it." For a community that has limited incomes there is an exchange of talents and commitment. For example, moms take turns doing child care to give other women time off, teaching sewing, or learning carpentry, or counselling each other's adolescents.

Another interesting aspect of the Gilbert Park Program is the opportunity it provides Ma Mawi Wi Chi Itata Centre.

The Ma Mawi Wi Chi Itata Centre has shifted from providing services to a community, to working with a community to co-create a healthy community and families. The shift involves moving away from "this is what we do" to "what do you need and how can we co-create something that will work." A prime example is their partnership with Correctional Services Canada. This partnership co-created the Family Violence Program Story Mountain Project. The primary objectives of this Project are: to stop and eliminate violence within intimate and family relationships; to have men accept full responsibility for their violent behaviours; and, to provide the opportunity for men to be exposed to teachings and practices which help them develop a positive cultural identity.

The program provides an environment in which men feel safe to disclose their personal stories, as well as alternatives in dealing with their feelings of anger and effects of violence in a manner that enhances their lives and their family members' lives. Through education, counselling, and a supportive environment, men are able to relieve their sense of isolation and increase their self-esteem.

Perhaps the best way to capture the care, commitment, and partnerships that occur in Gilbert Park is to share a letter from a constable who worked in the community for four years.

ON THE BEAT

It is with mixed emotions that I inform residents that I have sought and obtained a transfer from my present position to that of a Service Centre Officer to be located on McPhillips.

I have been fortunate to have worked in the neighbourhood I call home — first as a Community Officer and more recently Beat Officer. In all, I have worked in the area for four years. However my decision to seek change was to broaden my work experience to make me a better officer. Yes, old dogs can learn new tricks!!!

With my departure, I leave you in the capable hands of Constable Kevin Wiens. Kevin is a ten-year veteran who has held various positions with the police service which include uniform patrol, detectives, and beat officer. In addition another officer will be placed in the Tyndall Park area. These officers can be reached by leaving a message at ph# 986-7939.

Contact with me may not be lost. In the event you wish to report an incident (one not requiring police attend your home), you can now attend the new Service Centre located on McPhillips in Moore's Centre (next to Northgate Shopping Centre). In addition, accident reports and paying of parking fines may be made at this location. The hours of operation are 8:00 am to 8:00 pm — seven days a week. It is expected the office will open October 5th, 1998.

I will also continue providing Neighbourhood Watch information like in the past.

I like to think with residents of this neighbourhood, school staff, resource services, and police presence — we have made a difference. With the new officers in place, I very much believe this trend will continue.

My heartfelt thanks to everyone for making my job a little easier and very enjoyable.

Sincerely,

Craig Waterman
Constable #1233/3

William Whyte Community School

The purpose of the William Whyte Community School is to be a place for students, their families, and staff where the individual is cherished and the collective is celebrated. The school provides a learning environment where each person can reach his or her full potential and work together for community development.

This school clearly understands that underdeveloped people result in social costs. For example, in Manitoba, while native people make up 13 per cent of the population, 50 per cent are welfare cases, 78 per cent are apprehended and taken into care, and 78 per cent of the youth are in custody. While 63 per cent non-natives complete high school, only 30 per cent of natives complete high school. The number of native people below the poverty line is four times that of non-native people! Thus, this community school is addressing larger community issues of poverty, economic development, and social and emotional health through transformational education.

CODE OF CONDUCT FOR THE WINNIPEG SCHOOL DIVISION No. 1 BEHAVIOUR EXPECTATIONS AND CONSEQUENCES FOR STUDENTS, STAFF, PARENTS/GUARDIANS

No doubt the success of this community school is their clarity of values and their commitment to their values as expressed through daily actions. Staff, students, and families commit themselves to live a Code of Conduct. Their Code of Conduct defines expectations of behaviour for students, staff, and parents/guardians. Consequences for inappropriate behaviour are spelled out in the Code and are directed at correcting specific behaviours.

Below is the school's Code for students, staff, and parents/guardians.

Students

- Attend school regularly. Be on time, bring all required supplies and completed homework. When finished for the day, leave the school grounds promptly.
- Show common courtesy and respect to all; defiance of authority, abusive language, and aggressive behaviour are unacceptable at all times.
- Behave respectfully to all regardless of race, religion, gender, age, or sexual orientation.
- Solve conflicts peacefully through discussion or by seeking help.
- Dress appropriately for classes and activities.
- Respect school property and the property of others.
- Follow this Code of Conduct and any code that the school may have.
- Make the most of the time in school: strive for academic excellence through classroom participation.

Staff

- Provide the programs and services prescribed by the Winnipeg School Division and the Department of Education.
- Establish a positive learning environment.
- Evaluate students' achievement, and explain the evaluation

procedures to be used in each course.

- Keep students, parents/guardians and administration informed about student progress, attendance, and behaviour.
- Show common courtesy and respect to all; defiance of authority, abusive language, and aggressive behaviours are unacceptable at all times.
- Behave respectfully to all regardless of race, religion, gender, age, or sexual orientation.
- Treat students and other staff members fairly and consistently.
- Respect confidential information about students and staff.
- Dress appropriately for the working environment.
- Assist students in resolving conflicts peacefully and use the Code of Conduct to encourage appropriate behaviour.

Parents/Guardians

- Make sure your children attend classes regularly, arrive at school on time, and do their homework.
- Attend school events, support the school and stay in contact with school staff.
- Help your children develop positive attitudes to school and respect the staff and school property.
- Show common courtesy and respect to all; abusive language and aggressive behaviour are unacceptable at all times.
- Treat all individuals respectfully regardless of race, religion, gender, age, or sexual orientation.
- Encourage the peaceful resolution of conflict. Discourage violent or aggressive behaviour to solve a problem.
- Should there be a concern, try to solve it with your child's teacher. If unresolved, contact the principal. If the problem remains, then contact the superintendent. If the concern is not resolved at this level, then contact the Board of Trustees.
- Talk about the Code of Conduct with your children, and what it means.

The Code itself becomes an instrument of community development. The implementation and enforcement of the Code creates ample opportunity for teaching values to students, staff, and parents. The signed agreement sets the stage for conversation on the meaning of values and commitment to values. This approach is particularly congruent with the cultural values of the largely First Nations community. Living these values becomes the teaching, learning, and living challenge of this community school.

CODE OF CONDUCT - TO BE RETURNED TO:

_____
(Parent's Name)

I have read the William Whyte Community School Code of Student conduct. I have gone over it with my child. I will help to see that my child learns the Code and follows the expectations and rules of the school.

My child has agreed to follow the expectations and rules of William Whyte Community School.

_____
Date

_____
Signature of Parent/Guardian

_____
Signature of Student

Other comments (Optional)

Integrated Philosophy

The William Whyte Community School is an example of community partnerships. The community school project is a partnership involving the City of Winnipeg, Winnipeg Child and Family Services, and the Winnipeg School District. The intent is to integrate service providers to meet the educational, social, and health needs of community members. The idea is to learn together and to problem solve in order to assist each in reaching his or her full potential while working together.

The school hums day and night. The myriad activities

created by the community might include:

- Coffee Club
- Council Meetings
- Homework Club
- Reading Program
- Integrated Special Education classes
- Nutrition Breaks
- Breakfast Program
- Cultural Arts and Awareness
- Alternative School for Grade 8
- Family Pow Wow
- Volleyball

The school walls are alive with pictures of individuals and groups of community members. Expressions of talent are also posted on classroom and school walls. The computer room has children surfing the Net, making charts and graphs, or working reading and math programs.

The principal suggests that a community school needs to be a transformation experience. Not surprising then when a first grader walked in late and looking glum, the school secretary leaned into the hall and said, "Kevin, have a great day!" Transformational learning requires a radical rethinking of schools where attention is paid to the whole child, where there is care for the entire community, there is a challenge of the status quo of what can or cannot be done.

The critical perspective taken by the staff promotes being healthy, collective planning, levelled positions, collective contributions and involvement, a belief in "everyone matters," and value-based (not rule-based) decision making.

Meetings of the collective are held every second Friday and agendas focus on:

- ideas,
- what works and what doesn't, and
- being together and knowing each other.

The meetings are grounded in the belief that the community has the capacity to solve their own problems. Further, the problems are viewed as community problems and are framed as "We have a problem, who can help with this?"

The William Whyte Community School is only limited by economic resources. Most of what they do is done by pooling resources. However, while the school does some fund raising projects, schools are not in the economic development business; they are in the education business — transformation through education. A critical aspect of their success is the philosophy that "If we can find the money, we can do it." This is a good example of the need for different capitals, in this case economic capital, in order to create more social capital.

Andrews Street Family Centre

The history of the Andrews Street Family Centre is a statement of community development.

The Andrews Street Family Centre was developed following an intensive period of community consultation. Over a period of two years it brought together a number of existing community programs into one facility, combining them with new programs that together contribute to the development of a continuum of family supports serving all age groups. In 1994, a community survey and needs assessment was carried out. It focussed on identifying not only the unmet needs in the area, but also the neighbourhood resources and strengths that could be utilized.

The Centre, incorporated in February 1995, was initially sponsored by a partnership with representation from inner city schools and local resource groups, including William Whyte Community School, the Community Education Development Association (CEDA), Pritchard Place, the Nyinakawa School, the North End Women's Centre, the Native Women's Transition Centre, the Native Alcohol Foundation, and the local Child and Family Services office. In the summer of 1995, further discussion took place to broaden the range of family support services offered. This resulted in the expansion of the Centre through amalgamation with Pritchard Place Drop-In Centre and the Moms Helping Moms project. The Moms Helping Moms project is a community-based approach to providing outreach and support to adolescent parents which originally started in response to issues identified by the Family Violence Support Group and Hope Health Care Centre. Pritchard Place Drop-In Centre, which had been operating separately for eight years, serves children aged 6-17 years old. It had been in decline because it had experienced a number of problems with gangs of youth who vandalized the premises and created a bad reputation. The coming together of the various groups revitalized the Pritchard Place Drop-In and brought the various programs together under one roof. The key principles guiding the plans for amalgamation included:

- a commitment to maintain and enhance existing and new programs and services for children aged 1-17 years and their families.
- a willingness to more fully develop a community-based service delivery model that de-emphasized professional direction and facilitated community action and empowerment.
- an intention to reduce administrative overhead and to utilize all resources in a more cost-effective manner.
- the creation of a new organization that would make the most effective use of volunteer/board participation.

Programs In Action

The Centre has a comprehensive program that addresses parent education and support, family preservation, child care and child development, health education and care, youth development, employment and economic development, community development, leadership, and advocacy.

- **Parent-child drop-in:** offers parents and caregivers laundry and phone facilities, information about community resources, and a place for coffee. Children are cared for in a separate play group in the children's program area.
- **Parenting classes:** supported by Moms Helping Moms outreach staff and City of Winnipeg public

health nurses. Parenting classes include sessions on Nobody's Perfect and 1-2-3 Magic (a course designed to help parents with child management and appropriate discipline).

- **Single fathers group:** held on a weekday afternoon for men who wish to share their parenting experiences and concerns.
- **Weekly newsletter and monthly calendar:** are also published to share information about local events, as well as articles about various aspects of child and family life, health, and wellbeing.
- **Sharing circles:** led by a First Nations elder, for men, women and youth, provides a place for people to talk, share experiences, and promote healing.
- **Free workshops:** on a variety of topics, based on requests from the community or demonstrated need, for example, welfare rights, woodworking, soapstone carving, smoking cessation, breast self-examination. Child care is provided. These workshops are advertised in the weekly school newsletter.
- **Moms Helping Moms program:** aims to reach out to at-risk teen parents who are not linked up with other helping services or systems and thereby prevent family crises and breakup. The approach represents a shifting of resources and service responses from more formal, professionally designated diagnosis and intervention strategies, to one of practical, personal, community-based support. Four community women who had been trained as outreach/support workers were hired by ASFC to provide home visiting, peer support and mentoring to young mothers. The reason for this shift is that adolescent mothers and their children, who face the greatest risk of poverty and dependency on social services, often lack the experience, the opportunities, and the practical personal supports they would require to plan for and work towards greater self reliance.
- **School-based outreach and family support services:** based at William Whyte Community School, a family support worker and a community outreach

worker focus on prevention and on averting the need for more formal social service intervention. They offer counselling and support services to children and families, assist in organizing committees to address local issues and plan special events. Funding for this school-based project is provided by the United Way of Winnipeg and Winnipeg Child and Family Services.

- **Mental health family support worker:** works out of Andrews Street Family Centre four days a week to provide consultation, counselling, play and family therapy, and referral to speech therapy and other mental health services as required. The position is funded by the Manitoba Adolescent Treatment Centre.

- **Children's program area:** offers a range of developmental and educational supports including arts and crafts, and introduction to reading. A nutritious snack is provided to all the children.

- **Oshki-Majahitowiin child development program:** is an early childhood education program guided by Aboriginal culture and tradition that is funded under the federal Aboriginal Head Start Initiative which provides both start-up and operational funding. The program serves approximately 40 children, aged 2-5 years, in two licensed half-day child development programs, one serving Cree children and the other serving Ojibway children. Breakfast and lunch are also provided. The Home-based Coordinator makes home visits to families who are on the waiting list or enrolled in the child development program. Through this "nesting" or home-visiting support program, families receive information, resources, support, and referral to other programs as needed. Parents are required to volunteer/participate in various aspects of the program for ten hours a month. Program links have been developed with the City of Winnipeg Public Health Department, Winnipeg School Division Number 1, the Child Guidance Clinic, and Winnipeg Child and Family Services. The goals of Oshki-Majahitowiin are to:

- establish and maintain a language- and culturally-based early childhood learning centre for children and their families in the Andrews Street area;
- develop and maintain a home-visiting program as a support service to the program and to the children and the families in the community;
- include parents/guardians, extended family members, elders, and community members in all aspects of the program;
- incorporate a community development focus in working cooperatively with other community organizations;
- develop and maintain high standards and quality of programs and services that protect the health and physical wellbeing and respect the individual rights of the children and families who use the Centre; and
- develop the human resource potential of the families who reside in the Andrews Street area.

Five community women and one man have been hired and trained in early childhood education at Red River Community College. Parents, guardians, extended family members, and elders are seen as integral to their children's early education; they are included in all aspects of the program and take part in the advisory committee.

- **Well-Child Clinic:** staffed by the City of Winnipeg public health nurses, the weekly clinic is offered on-site.
- **Prenatal classes:** are offered one afternoon a week by Andrews Street staff, in collaboration with public health nurses from the City of Winnipeg and a nutritionist the Mount Carmel Health Clinic. In addition to offering information and preparation for childbirth, the program staff are involved in initial post-natal follow-up when the babies are born.
- **Community kitchen:** provided opportunities for groups of mothers, fathers, and other caregivers to get together, plan meals, shop, and participate in two cooking days a week. The kitchen provides a relaxed environment where parents can stretch their food budget, take home nutritious foods, and learn new recipes.

- **Food-buying club:** is operated as a small store in the Centre by community residents; membership in the club is free. Basic foodstuffs, household and personal supplies are sold at cost. Products are also packaged in small quantities, so that they cost less and are made more accessible to people with limited incomes. Community residents also gain work experience in operating a cash register, in managing stock and inventory procedures, and in learning basic bookkeeping skills.
- **Food Bingo programs:** are offered from time-to-time to help with nutrition education. Participants play bingo to earn food prizes.
- **Clothing exchange:** used clothing is available at the Family Centre.
- **Laundry facilities:** a washer and dryer are available for community use.
- **Telephone access:** a telephone located in a quiet, private space is available to families who cannot afford their own.
- **Pritchard Place Drop-in Centre:** has been operating since 1986 and provides recreational, educational, and cultural activities for children and youth aged 6-17 years. Activities include movie and gym nights, arts and crafts, cooking classes, formal babysitting courses, community clean-up and mural painting, and sports. Parents are welcome and encouraged to participate along with their children. As a result of the amalgamation, the drop-in space has been renovated and changed from a separate drop-in centre into an integral part of the family resource centre. Funding is provided by the United Way of Winnipeg, Winnipeg Child and Family Services, and the City of Winnipeg.
- **Leadership Circle summer employment project:** the Drop-in participates in this Rotary Club project which provides youth with a $200 honorarium for taking part in community work such as helping senior citizens with small projects, cutting grass, and community clean-up.
- **Training and hiring of community residents to**

staff the Centre: while professional staff were originally involved in the setting up of some programs, their positions were not viewed as being permanent. There has been a planned transfer of key jobs to community people. Local residents now assume the majority of staff positions and directly participate in the planning and delivery of all aspects of service. For example, the present Executive Director, the Volunteer Coordinator, the Moms Helping Moms Coordinator, and most of the Head Start staff are community residents who have been trained/mentored to assume their current positions.

- **Integrated Approach to Health Action:** funded by Health Canada; encompasses three employment-related programs:
  - *Catering co-operative business:* employs one half-time staff and three community members on a casual basis who provide catering services to various groups. The employees also participate in training sessions that teach skills in business management.
  - *Workers' co-operative to support housing repairs:* the program coordinator works with other local agencies to develop strategies to provide housing in the community. A proposal is being developed to provide training for 15 local residents in house renovation.
  - *Adult upgrading and literacy leading to employment:* 20 adult students are involved in upgrading and Grade 12 equivalency programs which are offered at the William Whyte Community School.

- **Volunteers:** over 35 community volunteers in various aspects of the program whose work is facilitated by a volunteer coordinator. In a number of instances volunteers who demonstrate promise and motivation are encouraged to take part in various training opportunities; in time they may be hired to work in some aspect of the program.

Learn By Doing

The philosophy of the Centre is to engage volunteers in a process of learning-by-doing and through the learning, be empowered to work. The 33 staff and 40 volunteers interact daily in this learn-by-doing process. One woman who brought her kid to the day care described her learning as follows:

> "It changed my whole life. I brought my kid to day care and learned how to be a better parent. First I was a volunteer. Then I became involved in the council, hot dog day, got my husband involved, and eventually went back to school and got my B.A. I learned that I was smart and had skills."

Another woman said it this way:

> "My life was unsafe. There was gang violence, drugs, and prostitution. Things were out of control. Now I like what I am doing and I believe in what I am doing. Here I can bring my heart and head to work. These people are my family."

Another said:

> "I wouldn't go there (Manitoba Child and Family Services). I can't live with their mandate. There I had to go where the system wanted me to go and do what they wanted me to do. Here I learned about child care, to read and write, to like myself and how to create safety. Here my pay is not deducted when I have a doctor's appointment. When I have a doctor's appointment, I work harder!"

The invitations to get involved in the programs are an excellent statement of what they are up to and hoping to achieve. Black on white, simple brochures are used to "get out the word" about the drop-in centre, parenting classes, family centre, head start and so on. These brochures (rather than slick, multicolored brochures) communicate that real and down-to-earth people will be at the Centre to help. All are welcome and all will fit in. This is a place where you can come and get a meal and a clean shirt, or just wash your shirt. Here you can get support, learn how to cook, and belong. This Centre is addressing personal mastery or building human capital at a very basic level. At the same time it promotes and allows for some to literally break through concrete ceilings.

The Centre's approach is directed at accomplishing the following goals:

- to establish and operate a family-oriented, neighbourhood resource centre that can provide meaningful support for local residents;
- to contact and reach out to neighbourhood residents, particularly parents and their children, and encourage them to become involved in the activities and ownership of the Centre; and
- to develop ways that neighbourhood residents can rely on their own initiatives and reduce the need for outside "professional" intervention.

Rossbrook House

Two postal code areas which represent the lowest economic areas in Canada are located in downtown Winnipeg. In this location of increased poverty are a number of community initiatives which serve and work against the hopelessness of poverty, isolation, and oppression. These initiatives help make dreams come true. These are their stories.

Rossbrook House

Rossbrook House is a home away from home. It is open seven days a week and offers flexible programming to meet the needs of the ever changing neighbourhood. Floor hockey, basketball, movies, bingo, pizza, pool, arts and crafts, badminton, and ice hockey are offered within this shelter and place of safety.

Twenty-four staff, a board of directors, and numerous volunteers live within the community and foster an environment of safety, comfort, and respect.

Rossbrook's Goals

Rossbrook is a neighbourhood centre serving children, adolescents, and young adults. Rossbrook offers a constant alternative to the destructive environment of the streets.

Rossbrook employs the principles of self-help and self-referral. The staff are drawn from among the ranks of the regular attendees — young people living in the local area interested in building better lives for themselves, their neighbours, and their friends.

The principles and practices of Rossbrook are well expressed in God's response to the prophet Micah:

> What is required of us is simply this
> - to act justly
> - to love tenderly
> - and to walk humbly with our God.

Such is the goal, and dream, and the persistent endeavour of Rossbrook House.

Philosophy and Commitment to Education

Rossbrook House has three alternative school programs which operate with the cooperation of Winnipeg School Division No 1. These programs provide solid, individualized, academic instruction, with a wide range of cultural, social, recreational, and athletic activities. The programs build on individual strengths in a comfortable and welcoming environment:

- WI WABIGOONI is an elementary program which began in 1981. It is an off-site program of Victoria Albert School.
- EAGLES' CIRCLE is a junior-high program which began in 1977 and remains as an off-site program of Hugh John MacDonald School.
- RISING SUN is located at Elgin House. It is an high school that began in 1982 and is administered by R.B. Russell Vocational School.

The educational philosophy is one of building on the strengths of the individual through education. Through learning they have the opportunity to re-experience their competencies and capacity. They are repeatedly offered an opportunity "to do their best with the cards dealt them that day." The key to their work is creating relationships which provide "connections." Connections are the locations of opportunities for Rossbrook staff and volunteers. The starting point is "hire the kids." Once hired, the kids have the commitment of the staff and volunteers to co-create.

A man over 30 years of age, who moved out of his home at 15, expressed his experience this way:

> "I was getting into trouble. The streets were not a good place for me. I was told if I showed up everyday I would get $50 a month spending money. I was doing my work and getting ahead. I've learnt plenty: maintenance and repair, carpentry, group work, people skills, crime prevention, about abuse and I've attended conferences on 'anything.' It's a unique place. No other place like it. It's a safe place. I try to make it safe for others."

In their 1997 annual report, Sister Lesley Sacouman and Sister Bernadette O'Reilly captured the spirit of Rossbrook House by quoting Oriah Mountain Dreamer, an Indian Elder.

> "It doesn't interest me to know where you live or how much money you have. I want to know if you can get up after the night of grief and despair, weary and bruised to the bone, and do what needs to be done for the children."

Their commitment to doing what needs to be done for the children is evidenced through their capacity to rise above professional boundaries and focus on the larger community issue of poverty. Their commitment to overcoming poverty through education in the context of personal relations, is a prime example of how to build social capital. Their focus on the issue is clear, their commitment takes the form of action, and they embrace, include, and involve the larger community in their dream. Anyone who wants to overcome their circumstances or the circumstances of the community can live the dream.

Argyris, C. (1991). Teaching Smart People How to Learn. <u>Harvard Business Review</u>, <u>1991</u>(May-June), 99-109.

Argyris, C. (1992). <u>On Organizational Learning</u>. Cambridge, MA: Blackwell Publishers, Inc.

Argyris, C. (1994). Good Communication that Blocks Learning. <u>Harvard Business Review</u>, <u>1994</u>(July-August), 151.

Argyris, C., & Schon, D. (1974). <u>Theory In practice: increasing professional effectiveness</u>. San Fransisco: Jossey-Bass Publishers.

Astley, G. W., & Fombrun, C. J. (1983). Collective strategy: Social ecology of organizational environments. <u>Academy of Management Review, 8,</u> 576-587.

Atlee, T. (1998). <u>Dialogue</u>. The Co-Intelligence Institute. <u>http://www.best.com/ ~cil/P-dialogue.html</u>.

Atlee, T. (1998) <u>Wholeness, interconnectedness and co-creativity</u>. The Co-Intelligence Institute. <u>http://www.best.com/~cii/I-whole interconn cocreatv.html</u>,

Banerjee, A. V. (1997). A theory of misgovernance. <u>Quarterly Journal of Economics</u>, 1289.

Bellefeuille, G., Garrioch, S., & Ricks, F. (1997). <u>Breaking the rules: transforming governance in social services</u>. Thompson, Manitoba: Awasis Agency of Northern Manitoba.

Bish, R. (1974). Urban health, education and welfare programs in a federal system. In S. Mushkin (Ed.), <u>State aids for human services in a federal system</u> . Georgetown: Georgetown University.

Bish, R. (1996). <u>Amalgamation: Is it the solution?</u> Paper prepared for The Coming Revolution in Local Government conference .

Bish, R., & Ostrom, V. (1979). <u>Understanding urban government — Metropolitan reform reconsidered (Domestic affairs study 20)</u>. Washington, DC: American Enterprise Institute for Public Policy.

Block, P. (1996). <u>Stewardship: Choosing service over self-interest.</u> San Francisco: Berrett-Koehler Publishers.

Bohm, D. (1980). <u>Wholeness and the implicate order</u>. London: Routledge & Kegan Paul.

Boix, C., & Posner, D. N. (1998). Social capital: explaining its origins and effects on government performance. <u>British Journal of Political Science,</u> <u>28</u>(4), 686-688.

Borgos, S., & Douglas, S. (1996). Community organizing and civic renewal: A view from the South. <u>Social Policy,</u> (Winter), 18-28.

Brehm, J., & Rahn, W. (1997). Individual-level evidence for the causes and consequences of social capital. <u>American Journal of Political Science,</u> <u>41</u>(3), 999-1023.

Briggs, X. D. (1997). Social capital and the cities: Advice to change agents. <u>National Civic Review,</u> <u>86</u>(2), 110-117.

Bruner, C. (1996). <u>Realizing a vision for children, families and neighbourhoods: an alternative to other modest proposals</u> . National Center for Service Integration.

Burt, R. S. (1997). The contingent value of social capital. <u>Administrative Science Quarterly</u>, <u>42</u>(2), 339-365.

Chapin, R. K. (1995). Social policy development: The strengths perspective. <u>Social Work</u>, <u>40</u>, 506-514.

Chawla, S., & Renesch, J. E. (1995). <u>Learning organizations: developing cultures for tomorrow's workplace</u>. Portland, Oregon: Productivity Press.

Checkoway, B. (1997). Core concepts for community change. <u>Journal of Community Practice</u>, <u>4</u>(1), 11-29.

Christensen, C. M. (1997). Making strategy: Learning by doing. <u>Harvard Business Review</u>, <u>75</u>(6), 141-156.

Civic Partners. (1996). <u>Building social trust — A blueprint for building social trust</u>. Pew Partnership for Civic Change.

Civic Practices Network. (1998). <u>Social Capital.</u> <u>http:// fount.journalism.wisc.edu/cpn/sections/tools/models/social_capital.html</u>.

Coleman, J. S. (1988). Social capital in the creation of human capital. <u>American Journal of Sociology</u>, <u>94 </u>(Supplement), S95-S120.

Coleman, J. S. (1994/1995). Redesigning American public education. <u>On the Horizon</u>, <u>3</u>(2), 1-2, 5.

Community Care and Public Health SW/SE Networks. (1997). <u>Community capacity building & asset mapping: model summary</u> . Edmonton, Alberta: Community Development.

Daloz, L. A. (1986). <u>Effective teaching and mentoring</u>. San Fransisco: Jossey-Bass Publishers.

De Geus, A. P. (1988). Planning as learning. <u>Harvard Business Review</u>, <u>1988</u>(March-April), 70-74.

De Souza Briggs, X. (1997). Social Capital and the cities: Advice to change agents. National Civic Review, 86(2), 111-117.

Diani, M. (1997). Social movements and social capital: A Network perspective on movement outcomes. An International Journal, 2(2), 129-147.

Dunlop, K. E. (1995). The best interests test in the Child and Family Services Act of Manitoba — in whose best interests? Paper presented at the Freedom to Change Conference, Elkhorn Resort.

Evans, P. (1996). Government action, social capital and development: Reviewing the evidence on synergy. World Development, 24(6), 1119-1132.

Flora, C. B. (1995, Fall, 1995). Social capital and sustainability: Agriculture and communities in the Great Plains and Corn Belt. Sustainable Agriculture Newsletter.

Flower, J. (1994). Community assessments: Five perspectives. Healthier communities action kit, Module 3 . Los Angeles, CA: The Healthcare Forum.

Flower, J. (1994). How change works in building healthy communities: Four observations. Healthier communities action kit, Module 3 . Los Angeles, CA: Healthcare Forum.

Flower, J. (1994). How to build a healthy community. Healthier communities action kit, Module 3 . Los Angeles, CA: The Healthcare Forum, Leadership Strategies for Healthcare.

Flower, J. (1994). Local action. Healthier communities action kit, Module 4. Los Angeles, CA: Healthcare Forum.

Flower, J. (1995). Collaboration: The new leadership. The Healthcare Forum Journal, 38(6).

Flower, J. (1996). Aiken, South Carolina: A case study of community transformation. Emerging best practices in partnerships to improve health . Los Angeles, CA: The Healthcare Forum.

Flower, J. (1996). Bethel New Life, Chicago: A case study of community transformation. <u>Emerging best practices in partnerships to improve health</u>. Los Angeles, CA: The Healthcare Forum.

Flower, J. (1996). Mesa County, Colorado: A case study of community transformation. <u>Emerging best practices in partnerships to improve health</u>. Los Angeles, CA: The Healthcare Forum.

Flower, J. (1996). Orlando, Florida: A case study of community transformation. <u>Emerging best practices in partnerships to improve health</u>. Los Angeles, CA: The Healthcare Forum.

Fountain, J. E. (1997). Social capital: A key enabler of innovation. In L. M. Branscomb & J. H. Keller (Eds.), <u>Investing innovation: creating a research and innovation policy that works</u>. Boston: MIT Press.

Fox, J. (1997). <u>The World Bank and social capital: contesting the concept</u>. University of California.

Freire, P. (1973). <u>Education for critical consciousness</u>. Cambridge, Massachusetts: The Continuum Publishing Corporation.

Freire, P. (1984). <u>Pedagogy of the oppressed</u>. New York: The Continuum Publishing Corporation.

Freire, P. (1985). <u>The politics of education: Culture, power, and liberation</u>. South Hadley, Massachusetts: Bergin & Garvey Publishers, Inc.

Freire, P., & Faundez, A. (1992). <u>Learning to question: A pedagogy of liberation</u>. New York: The Continuum Publishing Company.

Fries, D. M., & Kruse, R. A. (1995). <u>Leading learning communities: a case study of organizational learning at EDS</u>, MIT.

Fukuyama, F. (1995). <u>Trust</u>. The Free Press.

Garvin, D. A. (1993). Building a Learning Organization. <u>Harvard Business Review</u>, <u>1993</u>(July-Aug), 78-91.

Goleman, D. (1995). <u>Emotional intelligence</u>. New York: Bantam.

Goleman, D. (1998). <u>Working with emotional intelligence</u>. New York: Bantam.

Green, G. P. (1996). <u>Social capital and entrepreneurship: Bridging the family and community</u>. Paper presented at the Cornell University Conference on the Entrepreneurial Family — Building Bridges, New York City.

Gulati, P. & Guest, G. (1990). The community-centered model: A garden-variety approach or a radical transformation of community practice? <u>Social Work</u>, <u>35</u>(1), 63-68.

Gummer, B. (1998). Social relations in an organizational context: Social capital, real work, and structural holes. <u>Administration in Social Work</u>, <u>22</u>(3), 87-105.

Hamner, C. (1996). Interview with Frances Hesselbein President of the Drucker Foundation for Nonprofit Management. <u>Civic Partners</u>, (Spring).

Hargreaves, A. (1996). Transforming knowledge: Blurring the boundaries between research, policy, and practice. <u>Educational Evaluation and Policy Analysis</u>, <u>18</u>(2), 105-122.

Harri-Augstein, S., & Thomas, L. F. (1991). <u>Learning conversations: The self-organised learning way to personal and organisational growth</u>. London: Routledge.

Heller, K. (1989). The return to community. <u>American Journal of Community Psychology</u>, <u>17</u>(1), 1-15.

Henderson, H. (1994). <u>Healthier communities and "economism"</u>. Los Angeles, CA: Healthcare Forum, Leadership Strategies for Healthcare.

Herrick, J. (1995). <u>Empowerment practice and social change: The place for new social movement theory</u>. Seattle, WA: University of Washington. <u>http://wever.u.washington.edu/~jamesher/herrick.htm</u>.

Illich, I., Zola, I. K., McKnight, J., Caplan, J., & Shaiken, H. (1977). <u>Disabling professions</u>. New York: Marion Boyars.

Isaacs, W. N. (1993). Taking Flight: Dialogue, Collective Thinking, and Organizational Learning. Organizational Dynamics, 1993(Autumn), 24-39.

Isaacs, W. N. (1997). The Dialogue Project Annual Report 1993-94. http://www.sol-ne.org:80/res/wp/8004.html

Jaworski, J. (1996). Synchronicity — The inner path of leadership. San Francisco: Berrett-Koehler Publishers.

Kadlecek, J. M. (1997). Cooperation Among Local Governments. National Civic Review, 86(2), 175.

Kawachi, I., Kennedy, B. P., Lochner, K., & Prothow-Stith, D. (1997). Social capital, income inequality and mortality. American Journal of Public Health, 87(9), 1491-1498.

Keating, D. P. (1995). The learning society in the information age. In S. A. Rosell (Ed.), Changing maps: Governing in a world of rapid change (pp. 205-229). Ottawa, Ontario: Carleton University Press.

Kenny, S. (1996). Contestations of community development in Australia. School of Social Inquiry, Deakin University.

Kim, D. H. (1993). The Link between Individual and Organizational Learning. Sloan Management Review, 1993(Fall), 37-49.

Kleiner, A., & Roth, G. (1997). How to Make Experience Your Company's Best Teacher. Harvard Business Review, 75(5), 172-177.

Knack, S., & Keefer, P. (1997). Does social capital have an economic payoff? — A cross-country investigation. The Quarterly Journal of Economics (November), 1251-1287.

Kofman, F., & Senge, P. M. (1995). Communities of commitment: The heart of learning organizations. In S. Chawla & J. Renesch (Eds.), Learning organizations: developing cultures for tomorrow's workplace (pp. 14-43). Portland, OR: Productivity Press.

Korbin, J. E., & Coulton, C. J. (1996). The role of neighbors and the government in neighborhood-based child protection. <u>Journal of Social Issues</u>, <u>52</u>(3), 163-176.

Kretzmann, J. P., & McKnight, J. L. (1993). <u>Building communities from the inside out: a path toward finding and mobilizing a community's assets.</u> Chicago: John Kretzmann and John McKight.

Kreuter, M., Lezin, N., & Baker, B. (1998). <u>Is social capital a mediating structure for effective community-based health promotion?</u> Paper prepared for Health 2000 conference. Atlanta, GA.

Langer, E. J. (1997). <u>The power of mindful learning.</u> Reading, MA: Addison-Wesley.

Lappe, F. M., & Du Bois, P. M. (1995). <u>The quickening of America – Rebuilding our nation, remaking our lives.</u> San Francisco: Jossey-Bass.

Lappe, F. M., & Du Bois, P. M. (1997). Building social capital without looking backward. <u>National Civic Review</u>, <u>86</u>(2), 119-128.

Lave, J., & Wenger, E. (1991). <u>Situated learning: Legitimate peripheral participation</u>. Cambridge: Cambridge University Press.

Leeder, S. (1998). <u>Social capital and its relevance to health and family policy</u>. Paper presented at the Federal Government Health and Family Services Policy Forum.

Lemann, N. (1996). Kicking in groups. <u>Atlantic Monthly</u>, <u>277</u>(4), 22-26.

Levitt, B., & March, J. G. (1988). Organizational learning. <u>Annual Review of Sociology</u>, <u>14</u>, 319-340.

Limerick, D., Passfield, R., & Cunnington, B. (1994). Towards an action learning organization. <u>The Learning organization</u>, <u>1</u>(2), 29-40.

Loury, G. C. (1997). How to mend affirmative action. <u>The Public Interest</u>. (Spring), 33-43.

Maser, C. (1997). <u>Sustainable community development: Principles and concepts</u>. Delray Beach, Florida: St. Lucie Press.

Mattox, W. R., Jr. (1995). The one-house schoolroom: The extraordinary influence of family life on student learning. <u>Family Policy</u>, <u>8</u>(4).

McGill, M. E., & Slocum, J. W. J. (1993). Unlearning the Organization. <u>Organizational Dynamics</u>, <u>1993</u>(Autumn), 67-78.

McKnight, J. (1997). A 21st-century map for healthy communities and families. <u>Families in Society</u>, (March/April), 117-127.

McKnight, J.L. (1995). <u>The careless society: Community and its counterfeits</u>. New York: Basic Books.

McKnight, J. L., & Kretzmann, J. (1998) <u>Mapping Community Capacity</u>. IPR Publications. <u>http://www.nwu.edu/IPR/publications/mcc.html</u>

McMillan, D. W., & Chavis, D. M. (1986). Sense of community: A definition and theory. <u>Journal of Community Psychology</u>, <u>14</u>(1), 6-23.

Mezirow, J. (1991). <u>Transformative Dimensions of Adult Learning.</u> San Francisco: Jossey-Bass Publishers.

Mezirow, J. (1991). Transformation Theory and Cultural Context: A Reply to Clark and Wilson. <u>Adult Education Quarterly</u>, <u>41</u>(3), 188-192.

Miller, R. (1997). Healthy Boston and social capital: application, dynamics and limitations. <u>National Civic Review</u>, <u>86</u>(2), 157-162.

Morse, S. W. (1996). Creating social trust: An essay on building new looms. <u>Civic Partners</u>, (Spring). <u>http://www.cpn.org/pew_partnership/ civic_partners1.html</u>.

Ostrom, E. (1990). <u>Governing the commons — The evolution of institutions for collective action</u>. Cambridge: Cambridge University Press.

Ostrom, E. (1992). <u>Crafting institutions for self-governing irrigation systems</u>. San Francisco: Institute for Contemporary Studies.

Ostrom, E. (1997). A behavioral approach to the rational choice theory of collective action: presidential address to the American Political Science Association. <u>American Political Science Review</u>, <u>92</u>(1), 1-23.

Ostrom, V. (1973). <u>The intellectual crisis in American public administration</u>. University, AL: The University of Alabama Press.

Ostrom, V. (1987). <u>The political theory of the compound republic — Designing the American experiment</u>. Lincoln, NE: University of Nebraska Press.

Pascale, R., Millemann, M., & Gioja, L. (1997). Changing the way we change: How leaders at Sears, Shell, and the U.S. Army transformed attitudes and behavior — and made the changes stick. <u>Harvard Business Review</u>, <u>75</u>(6), 126-139.

Pine, B. A., Warsh, R., & Maluccio, A. N. (1998). Participatory management in a public child welfare agency: A key to effective change. <u>Administration in Social Work</u>, <u>22</u>(1).

Portes, A., & Landolt, P. (1996). The downside of social capital. <u>The American Prospect</u>, <u>94</u>(26), 18-21.

Portney, K. E., & Berry, J.M. (1997). Mobilizing minority communities: Social capital and participation in urban neighborhoods. <u>American Behavioral Scientist</u>, <u>40</u>(5), 632-644.

Potapchuk, W. R., Crocker, J. P., & Schechter, W. H., Jr. (1997). Building community with social capital: chits and chums or chats with change. <u>National Civic Review</u>, <u>86</u>(2), 129-139.

Putnam, R. D. (1993). The prosperous community: Social capital and public life. <u>The American Prospect</u>, <u>13</u>(Spring), 35-42.

Putnam, R. D. (1995). Bowling alone: America's declining social capital. <u>Journal of Democracy</u>, <u>6</u>(1), 65-78.

Putnam, R. D. (1996). The decline of civil society: How come? So what? <u>The Journal of Public Sector Management</u>, <u>27</u>(1).

Putnam, R. D. (1996). The strange disappearance of civic America. <u>The American Prospect</u>, <u>24</u>(Winter), 1-18.

Redhead, R. (1995). <u>Towards exclusive jurisdiction of child and family services</u>. Paper presented at the Freedom to Change Conference, Elkhorn Resort, Manitoba.

Ricks, F., & Charlesworth, J. (1998). <u>Creating healthy families and communities by building social capacity</u>. Paper presented at the School of Child and Youth Care 25th Anniversary, Victoria.

Roth, G. (1997). <u>Sustaining change by learning from collective experience</u>. Cambridge, MA: MIT Sloan School of Management.

Roth, G. L., & Senge, P. M. (1995). <u>From theory to practice: research territory, processes and structure at the MIT Center for Organizational Learning</u>. Cambridge, MA: Center for Organizational Learning, MIT Sloan School of Management.

Saleebey, D. (1996). The strengths perspective in social work practice: Extensions and cautions. <u>Social Work</u>, <u>41</u>, 296-305.

Saleebey, D. (1997). Community development, group empowerment, and individual resilience. In D. Saleebey (Ed.), <u>The strengths perspective in social work practice</u> (pp. 199-216). White Plains, NY: Longman.

Schein, E. H. (1993). On Dialogue, Culture, and Organizational Learning. <u>Organizational Dynamics</u>, <u>1993</u>(Autumn), 40-51.

Schein, E. (1997). <u>Three cultures of management: the key to organizational learning in the 21st century</u>. MIT: The Society for Organizational Learning. <u>http://learning.mit.edu/res/wp/10011.html</u>

Schwarz, R. M. (1994). <u>The skilled facilitator: Practical wisdom for developing effective groups</u>. San Fransisco: Jossey-Bass Publishers.

Secretan, L. (1997). <u>Reclaiming higher ground — Creating organizations that inspire the soul</u>. Toronto, Ontario: MacMillan Canada.

Senge, P. M. (1990a). <u>The fifth discipline: The art and practice of the learning organization</u>. New York: Currency Doubleday.

Senge, P. M. (1990b). The leader's new work: Building learning organizations. <u>Sloan Management Review</u> (Fall), 7-23.

Senge, P. M. (1998). <u>Making a better world</u>. MIT: The Society for Organizational Learning.<u>http://learning.mit.edu/res/kr/world.html</u>

Senge, P., Kleiner, A., Roberts, C., Ross, R., & Smith, B. (1994). <u>The Fifth Discipline Fieldbook: Strategies and Tools for Building a Learning Organization</u>. New York: Doubleday.

Shor, I., & Freire, P. (1987). <u>A pedagogy for liberation: Dialogues on transforming education</u>. South Hadley, Massachusetts: Bergin & Garvey Publishers, Inc.

Sirianni, C., & Friedland, L. (1998) <u>Social capital</u>. <u>http://fount.journalism.wisc.edu/cpn/sections/tools/models/social_capital.html</u>.

Sirianni, C., & Friedland, L. (1995). <u>Social capital and civic innovation: Learning and capacity building from the 1960s to the 1990s</u>. Paper presented at the American Sociological Association Annual Meetings, Washington, D.C. <u>http://www.journalism.wisc.edu/cpn/sections/new_citizenship/theory/socialcapital_civicinnov.html</u>

Skocpol, T. (1996). Unraveling from above. <u>The American Prospect</u>, (25), 20-25.

Smale, G.G. (1994). Integrating community and individual practice: A new paradigm for practice. In P. Adams and K. Nelson (Eds.), <u>Reinventing human services: Community- and family-centered practice</u> (pp. 59-80). New York: Aldine De Gruyter.

Smale, G.G. (1993). The nature and innovation of community-based practice. In E.E. Martinez-Brawley and S.M. Delevan (Eds.), <u>Transferring technology in the personal social services</u> (pp. 14-26). Washington, DC: NASW Press.

Smith, R. W. (1999). <u>Trusteeship: A summons to serve</u>. Center for Servant-Leadership. <u>http://greenleaf.org/trustees.html</u>.

Smith, S. R. (1997). Partnerships, community building and local government. <u>National Civic Review</u>, <u>86</u>(2), 167-173.

Sohng, S. S. L. (1995). <u>Participatory research and community organizing</u>. Paper presented at The New Social Movement and Community Organizing Conference, Seattle, WA.

Solow, R. M. (1997). <u>Learning from "Learning by Doing": Lessons for Economic Growth</u>. Stanford, CA: Stanford University Press.

Spears, L. (1996). Reflections on themes in servant-leadership. . Center for Servant-Leadership. <u>http://greenleaf.org/spears.html</u>.

Spears, L. (1998). Creating caring leadership for the 21st Century. <u>The Not-For-Profit CEO Monthly Letter</u>.

Spears, L. (1994). Servant leadership: Quest for caring leadership. <u>Inner Quest</u>, <u>1994</u>(2).

Sproule-Jones, M. H. (1975). <u>Public choice and federalism in Australia and Canada (Research Monograph No. 11)</u>. Canberra, Australia: Centre for Research on Federal-Financial Relations, The Australian National University.

Sproule-Jones, M. H. (1993). <u>Governments at work — Canadian parliamentary federalism and its public policy effects</u>. Toronto: University of Toronto Press.

St. John, W. (1998). Just what do we mean by community? — Conceptualizations from the field. <u>Health and Social Care in the Community</u>, <u>6</u>(2), 63-70.

Starhawk. Toward community: Structure and leadership in groups. In Starhawk <u>Truth or dare: Encounters with power, authority, and mystery</u> (pp. 256-295). San Fransisco: Harper and Row.

Sugarman, B. (1997). Notes towards a closer collaboration between organization theory, learning organizations and organizational learning in the search for a new paradigm. (pp. 1-24). Society for Organizational Learning.

Sullivan, W. P., & Rapp, C. A. (1994). Breaking away: The potential and promise of a strengths-based approach to social work practice. In R. G. Meinert, J. T. Pardeck, & W. P. Sullivan (Eds.), <u>Issues in social work: A critical analysis</u>. Westport, CT: Auborn House.

Sviridoff, M. & Ryan, W. (1997). Community-centred family service. <u>Families in Society, Mar/Apr</u>, 128-139.

Tullock, G. (1994). <u>The new federalist</u>. Vancouver, B.C.: The Fraser Institute.

Ulrich, D., Von Glinow, M. A., & Jick, T. (1993). High-impact learning: Building and diffusing learning capability. <u>Organizational Dynamics, 1993</u>(Autumn), 52-66.

Vaill, P. B. (1991). <u>Managing as a performing art</u>. San Fransisco: Jossey-Bass Publishers.

Walter, T. R. (1996). <u>Measuring community capacity building</u>. Washington, DC: Aspen Institute Rural Program. <u>www.aspenist.org/rural</u>.

Wandersman, A., Valois, R., Ochs, L., de la Cruz, D. S., Adkins, E., & Goodman, R. M. (1996). Toward a social ecology of community coalitions. <u>American Journal of Health Promotion, 10</u>(4), 299-307.

Watkins, K. E., & Marsick, V. J. (1993). <u>Sculpting the Learning Organization: Lessons in the Art and Science of Systemic Change</u>. San Fransisco: Jossey-Bass Publishers.

Weick, A., & Saleebey, D. (1995). Supporting family strengths: Orienting policy and practice toward the 21st Century. <u>Families in Society, 76</u>, 141-149.

Wharf-Higgins, J. (1997). Who participates?: Citizen participation in health reform in B.C. In B. Wharf & M. Clague (Eds.), <u>Community organizing: Canadian experiences</u> (pp. 273-301). Toronto, ON: Oxford University Press.

Willard, B. (1994). <u>Ideas on learning organizations: The "what", "why", "how" and "who"</u>. IBM Canada Ltd.

Wilson, P. (1997). Building social capital: A learning agenda for the twenty-first century. <u>Urban Studies</u>, <u>34</u>(5-6), 745-760.

World Bank (1996). Building community capacity. <u>The World Bank participation sourcebook, Chapter IV: Practice pointers in enabling the poor to participate</u>. Herndon, VA: The World Bank. <u>http://www.worldbank.org/html/edi/sourcebook/sb0403t.html</u>.